Strategic Motivations of Inward R&D FDI

"This new book makes an important and original contribution to the international business field. It provides a series of valuable new insights and ideas for scholars interested in advancing their research into the strategic motivations for inward FDI from different countries of origin to different host countries, focusing on the exploitation and creation of knowledge through foreign-based R&D. It should also prove a useful source of guidance for managers in MNEs and inward investment promotion agencies involved in determining the geographical division of knowhow-related capabilities and in influencing the international location of technology-related FDI."

—Grahame Fallon, *Brunel University, London, UK*

Osagie Igbinigie • Mark Cook
Lucy Zheng

Strategic Motivations of Inward R&D FDI

An Empirical Analysis of the UK

palgrave
macmillan

Osagie Igbinigie
Wolverhampton Business School
University of Wolverhampton
Wolverhampton, UK

Mark Cook
Wolverhampton Business School
University of Wolverhampton
Wolverhampton, UK

Lucy Zheng
Sheffield Business School
Sheffield Hallam University
Sheffield, UK

ISBN 978-3-030-41014-8 ISBN 978-3-030-41015-5 (eBook)
https://doi.org/10.1007/978-3-030-41015-5

This Palgrave Pivot imprint is published by the registered company Springer Nature Switzerland AG.
The registered company address is: Gewerbestrasse 11, 6330 Cham, Switzerland

Contents

About the Authors

Osagie Igbinigie is Lecturer in International Finance at the University of Wolverhampton. His research interests lie in the areas of motivations and impacts of inward and outward R&D-related FDI, focusing on advanced economies and comparing between OECD and non-OECD countries.

Mark Cook is Reader, International Business at the University of Wolverhampton. He has published extensively on FDI, focusing on aggregate inward UK determinants at both national and regional levels. His current research interests include FDI into the peripheral regions of the UK and comparative studies of African-inbound FDI.

Lucy Zheng is Professor of International Business Management at Sheffield Business School, Sheffield Hallam University. Her research interests lie widely in international business, management, economics, and entrepreneurship, with a core focusing on FDI and emerging markets.

List of Tables

1

Background and Research Rationale

Abstract MNEs operate in an increasingly competitive and complex environment. The quest for knowledge and technological competences has become vital for survival and prosperity. Although available evidence suggests that foreign R&D investments from advanced countries like the US, Japan, France, German, and the UK dominate the global stage, a growing number of MNEs have emerged from China, India, and Brazil. This chapter provides contexts with a comprehensive assessment of R&D internationalisation, inward R&D FDI in the UK and the economic geography of R&D globalisation. This chapter also provides specific research questions and research objectives addressed in this book.

Keywords R&D • FDI • MNE • Globalisation • Strategy • Motivation

O. Igbinigie et al., *Strategic Motivations of Inward R&D FDI*,
https://doi.org/10.1007/978-3-030-41015-5_1

R&D Internationalisation and R&D FDI in the UK

The UK, as a developed economy, is best placed to offer an innovative high-tech environment to support research-intensive activities. The national innovation base provides access to relevant localised research capabilities and innovative systems attractive for high-quality research (Cantwell et al. 2004; Cantwell and Mudambi 2005). The European Innovation Scoreboard 2018 ranked the UK the leader among EU member states on innovation. The ranking is based on the UK's best-performing indicators on excellent research systems and human resources. Equally to note is that multinational enterprises (MNEs) have an overwhelmingly positive and transformative effect on the UK economy. The UK host about 45,000 plus MNEs, which thus account for more than 13% of workforce employment (about 3 million workers) and 36% of the total turnover in the UK (Driffield et al. 2013). Recent data by the Office for National Statistics (ONS) of 40,000 UK companies show that foreign-owned firms in the UK are around 74% more productive than their domestic counterparts (ONS 2017). These, therefore, suggest that foreign affiliates play a vital role in the UK's technological development. Current UK R&D landscape shows that the UK is most appealing to MNEs for R&D activities compared to other top R&D performing states (DBIS 2016). For instance, the UK recorded about 44.3% of R&D performed by foreign-owned firms, compared to the US with about 14.3%, Japan 4.7%, Germany 26.2%, and France 22.1%. In terms of R&D foreign direct investment (FDI) in the UK, the US is the leading investor of UK's inward R&D, account for about 37% in 2016 (a decline from 45% in 2009). Behind the US are the Netherlands, Germany, France, and Japan occupying the second, third, fourth, and fifth position. The decline in US position could be as a result of the increase of inward R&D from other advanced countries as well as that from emerging markets (EMs). For example, Japan increased by 20%, Italy grew by 47%, South Africa increased by 48%, and Singapore increased by about 100%. The increase presences of MNEs' R&D activities in the UK corroborate with current phenomenon noted in the broader literature on R&D globalisation suggesting that MNEs operate in an increasingly competitive and complex environment. The growing number of MNEs from emerging markets (particularly from China, India, and Brazil) becoming internationally active performers and recipients of R&D (UNCTAD 2005; Gammeltoft 2006; Awate et al. 2015) raised fundamental questions among international business (IB) scholars as to what the motivations of R&D direct investments in a chosen location are (Von Zedtwitz and Gassmann 2002; Zheng and Tan 2011; Awate et al. 2015). The quest for knowledge and technological competences has become vital for survival and prosperity (Von Zedtwitz and Gassmann 2002; Cantwell and Mudambi 2005; Athukorala and Kohpaiboon 2010; Awate et al. 2015). It is well established in IB research that MNEs are attracted to locations that best fit the firm's technological specialisations (Blomström and Sjöholm 1999; Dunning 2002).

In a series of papers that are linked to traditional FDI motivations in the UK, authors have all shown that FDI is motivated to either exploit or augment home-based assets also known as strategic motivations of FDI (Driffield and Munday 2000; Driffield and Love 2005; Driffield et al. 2013). Asset-exploiting MNEs are more likely to generate technology and thus produce positive spillovers to domestic firms through linkage and/or externalities, whereas MNEs attracted to augment home-based assets are unlikely to generate significant productivity growth or technological transfer. From these existing studies, little is known empirically whether the strategic motivations of R&D FDI are subject to different specific motivations at the country level.

Pearce and Papanastassiou (1999) investigated the strategic evolution of MNEs by examining foreign labs in the UK. They revealed that foreign-owned R&D subsidiaries have metamorphosed from offering small-scale ad hoc support to local operations to playing a central role in the global strategies of the MNEs. Becker and Hall (2003) studied the role of exchange rate uncertainty and R&D FDI between the EU area and the UK. They showed that increases in the volatility of euro-dollar exchange rates tend to relocate R&D investment from the euro area into the UK. Griffith et al. (2004) examined foreign ownership and the UK's productivity in the service sector and R&D. They found that foreign MNEs in the UK have higher labour productivity than British MNEs in the production sector compared to the service sector, where British MNEs have higher labour productivity. They also revealed that foreign-owned MNEs conduct a substantial amount of British R&D. Cantwell and Mudambi (2005) used firm-level data from the UK-based subsidiaries of non-UK MNEs to investigate the difference between competence-creating and competence-exploiting subsidiary mandates. Cantwell and Mudambi (2005) found that the mandates of MNEs' R&D subsidiaries depend on the MNE group-level and subsidiary-level characteristics, as well as locational factors. Abramovsky et al. (2007) conducted an empirical study of the location choices of foreign-owned pharmaceutical R&D laboratories near UK university departments. They found that foreign-owned R&D laboratories co-locate near top-ranking chemistry departments. Higon (2007) investigated the impact of foreign R&D spillovers on total factor productivity (TFP) in UK manufacturing but failed to find empirical evidence that foreign R&D investment significantly affects manufacturing TFP. Harris and Li (2008) examined export propensity and export intensity using UK establishment-level data for R&D spending. They revealed that R&D spending has no significant impact on exporting behaviour after controlling for absorptive capacity. Extending this research stream, this current research, therefore, conducts a country-level empirical analysis examining the motivations of R&D FDI in the UK.

Cantwell and Iammarino (2000) described R&D FDI as the interdependence among foreign R&D units which constitute the MNE. Bloom and Griffith (2001) and Cincera et al. (2009) defined R&D FDI as R&D financed and performed by foreign affiliates of MNEs in host locations. Paoli and Guercini (1997) noted that the concept of "R&D internationalisation" is broader than that of "multinationalisation" because it includes other key elements (or mode of foreign investment entry) such as agreements, licenses, joint ventures, consortia, training of research personnel, and R&D cooperation with other entities or organisations. The globalisation of R&D according to Paoli and Guercini (1997) relates to the overall strategic behaviour of MNE foreign R&D activities. Paoli and Guercini (1997, p. 4) defined multinationalisation of R&D activities as consisting of the process of formation, development, and management of corporate research units in foreign locations. By these definitions, this study assumes that there is interdependency between the global (pool of R&D FDI in multiple locations) and local (pool of R&D FDI in a single location) networks of the MNE. In the economic geography for innovation, authors suggest that the question of global-local location choice relates to selected foreign locations that increase the firm-specific advantages (Von Zedtwitz and Gassmann 2002; Cantwell and Mudambi 2005; Awate et al. 2015). From the viewpoint of the host location, the question of global-local R&D units amplifies the focused trajectory of MNEs' networks for innovation and the causation of the trajectory which could set in motion (or reinforce) *virtuous and vicious circles* (Cantwell and Iammarino 2000; Khan et al. 2018). In the light of this, MNEs from developed economies should be favoured due to their access to capital, managerial, and technical know-how that could be embedded in different products produced by their foreign affiliates abroad (i.e. *virtuous circle*) (Wei and Liu 2001). As opposed to MNEs from less-developed economies (*vicious circle*) (with lesser managerial and technological capabilities transferred to host locations), which might spur little or no spillover effect on the host location (i.e. *vicious circle*). The consensus is that positive externalities from foreign affiliates create spillovers that could influence competition, productivity, and efficiency. Knowledge-intensive investments like R&D could increase technological innovativeness and knowledge stock in both the host and home locations (Cantwell et al. 2001; UNCTAD 2005). This research will build on previous studies by considering investing MNE' heterogeneity in economic and technological capabilities by grouping the study observations into Organization for Economic Co-operation and Development (OECD) countries and non-OECD countries.

Scholarly Debate on the Motivations of R&D FDI?

The bulk of the empirical studies exploring MNEs' R&D direct investment in foreign locations has mainly used subsidiary/firm-level data. Along these lines, scholarly studies have shown that MNEs are motivated to either create competences (home-based asset exploitation) or capture competences (home-based asset augmentation) by having portfolios of R&D networks in a single location and/or on a global level (Cantwell and Piscitello 2002; Von Zedtwitz and Gassmann 2002; Cantwell and Mudambi 2000, 2005; Awate et al. 2015). However, there is a lack of empirical studies exploring the location-specific motivations and its interactions in explaining the strategic motivations of R&D FDI. This current research, therefore, assumes that R&D FDI is similar to other traditional elements of the MNE (e.g. foreign production) and that it is likely to be driven by different motives. This draws support from Demirbag et al. (2007), Nieto and Rodríguez (2011), Zheng and Tan (2011), and Awate et al. (2015), who suggested that R&D FDI would have its distinctive location factors and that each location would respond with different factors. While this extant literature is rich on the strategic choice of R&D FDI, it is weak at offering a detailed structure on the similarity and distinction between strategic and specific motivations of R&D FDI. This incomplete knowledge prompts the need to conceptualise the motivations of R&D FDI. In response to this gap, this study aims to determine whether the twin strategic motivations of R&D FDI are subject to different specific motivations at the country level. Away from traditional FDI research, this study responds to authors that have called for empirical studies to examine other functional areas of MNE activities which could influence or change traditional determinants of FDI enshrined in the literature (Bardhan 2006; Fifarek and Veloso 2010; Nieto and Rodríguez 2011; Zhou 2016).

This study differs from previous studies that have examined the R&D FDI motivations within a specific country without considering whether and how different MNEs' technological configurations may lead to different specific motivations at the country level (Cantwell and Piscitello 2002; Von Zedtwitz and Gassmann 2002; Cantwell and Mudambi 2000, 2005; Awate et al. 2015). This study challenges current thinking in IB studies on the interplay between strategic motivations and location-specific motivations by shifting scholarly focus to the concentration of R&D FDI in a single location. The research aims to empirically examine the motivations of inward R&D FDI in the UK. This is achieved through the following research question:

- What are the strategic and specific motivations of inward R&D FDI into the UK, and by investing MNEs, grouped into OECD and non-OECD home countries?

  And the research objective:

- To empirically examine the strategic and specific motivations of inward R&D FDI into the UK, investigating the home countries grouped into OECD and non-OECD countries.

Conclusion

This chapter sets the scene by providing contexts with a comprehensive assessment of R&D FDI, the economic geography of R&D globalisation, and concentration of R&D FDI. The chapter provides specific research question and the research objectives addressed in this book.

References

Abramovsky, L., Harrison, R., & Simpson, H. (2007). University research and the location of business R&D. *The Economic Journal, 117*(519), 114–141.

Athukorala, P., & Kohpaiboon, A. (2010). Globalization of R&D by US-based multinational enterprises. *Research Policy, 39*(10), 1335–1347.

Awate, S., Larsen, M. M., & Mudambi, R. (2015). Accessing vs sourcing knowledge: A comparative study of R&D: Internationalization between emerging and advanced economy firms. *Journal of International Business Studies, 46*(1), 63–86.

Bardhan, A. D. (2006). Managing globalization of R&D: Organizing for offshoring innovation. *Human Systems Management, 25*(2), 103–114.

Becker, B., & Hall, S. G. (2003). *Foreign direct investment in industrial R&D and exchange rate uncertainty in the UK*. London: National Institute of Economic and Social Research.
Blomström, M., & Sjöholm, F. (1999). Technology transfer and spillovers: Does local participation with multinationals matter? *European Economic Review, 43*(4), 915–923.
Bloom, N., & Griffith, R. (2001). The internationalisation of UK R&D. *Fiscal Studies, 22*(3), 337–355.
Cantwell, J., & Iammarino, S. (2000). Multinational corporations and the location of technological innovation in the UK regions. *Regional Studies, 34*(4), 317–332.
Cantwell, J., Iammarino, S., & Noonan, C. (2001). *Sticky places in slippery space–the location of innovation by MNCs in the European regions*. Inward Investment Technological Change and Growth. Palgrave Macmillan: London.
Cantwell, J., & Mudambi, R. (2000). The location of MNE R&D activity: The role of investment incentives. *MIR: Management International Review, 40*(1), 127–148.
Cantwell, J., & Mudambi, R. (2005). MNE competence-creating subsidiary mandates. *Strategic Management Journal, 26*(12), 1109–1128.
Cantwell, J., & Piscitello, L. (2002). The location of technological activities of MNCs in European regions: The role of spillovers and local competencies. *Journal of International Management, 8*(1), 69–96.
Cantwell, J. A., Dunning, J. H., & Janne, O. E. (2004). Towards a technology-seeking explanation of US direct investment in the United Kingdom. *Journal of International Management, 10*(1), 5–20.
Cincera, M., Cozza, C., & Tübke, A. (2009, November 11–13). *The main drivers for the internationalization of R&D activities by EU MNEs*. Draft for the 4th Annual Conference of GARNET Network, IFAD.
Demirbag, M., Tatoglu, E., & Glaister, K. W. (2007). Dimensions of European direct investment activity in Turkey: Patterns and prospects. *International Journal of Emerging Markets, 2*(3), 274–297.
Department for Business Innovation and Skills (DBIS). (2016). *Innovation report 2016—Innovation, research and growth*. London: Department for Business Innovation and Skills.
Driffield, N., & Love, J. H. (2005). Who gains from whom? Spillovers, competition and technology sourcing in the foreign-owned sector of UK manufacturing. *Scottish Journal of Political Economy, 52*(5), 663–686.

Driffield, N., & Munday, M. (2000). Industrial performance, agglomeration, and foreign manufacturing investment in the UK. *Journal of International Business Studies, 31*(1), 21–37.

Driffield, N., Love, J., Lancheros, S., & Temouri, Y. (2013). *How attractive is the UK for future manufacturing foreign direct investment? Aston business school.* London: Foresight Government Office for Science.

Dunning, J. H. (2002). *Global capitalism, FDI and competitiveness.* Cheltenham: Edward Elgar Publishing.

Fifarek, B. J., & Veloso, F. M. (2010). Offshoring and the global geography of innovation. *Journal of Economic Geography, 10*(4), 559–578.

Gammeltoft, P. (2006). Internationalisation of R&D: Trends, drivers and managerial challenges. *International Journal of Technology and Globalisation, 2*(12), 177–199.

Griffith, R., Redding, S., & Van Reenen, J. (2004). Mapping the two faces of R&D: Productivity growth in a panel of OECD industries. *The Review of Economics and Statistics, 86*(4), 883–895.

Harris, R., & Li, Q. C. (2008). Exporting, R&D, and absorptive capacity in UK establishments. *Oxford Economic Papers, 61*(1), 74–103.

Higon, D. A. (2007). The impact of R&D spillovers on UK manufacturing TFP: A dynamic panel approach. *Research Policy, 36*(7), 964–979.

Khan, Z., Rao-Nicholson, R., & Tarba, S. Y. (2018). Global networks as a mode of balance for exploratory innovations in a late liberalizing economy. *Journal of World Business, 53*(3), 392–402.

Nieto, M. J., & Rodríguez, A. (2011). Offshoring of R&D: Looking abroad to improve innovation performance. *Journal of International Business Studies, 42*(3), 345–361.

Office for National Statistics (ONS). (2017). *UK foreign direct investment: Trends and analysis: Summer 2017.* Norwich: HMSO.

Paoli, M., & Guercini, S. (1997). *R & D Internationalisation in the strategic behaviour of the firm.* STEEP Discussion Paper, No 39.

Pearce, R., & Papanastassiou, M. (1999). Overseas R&D and the strategic evolution of MNEs: Evidence from laboratories in the UK. *Research Policy, 28*(1), 23–41.

UNCTAD. (2005). *Transnational corporations and the internationalization of R&D.* UNCTAD World Investment Report. Geneva: United Nations Publication.

Von Zedtwitz, M., & Gassmann, O. (2002). Market versus technology drive in R&D internationalization: Four different patterns of managing research and development. *Research Policy, 31*(4), 569–588.
Wei, Y., & Liu, X. (2001). *Foreign direct investment in China: Determinants and impact.* Cheltenham: Edward Elgar Publishing.
Zheng, P., & Tan, H. (2011). Home economy heterogeneity in the determinants of China's inward foreign direct investment. *Transnational Corporations, 20*(2), 1–29.
Zhou, Y. (2016). Drivers of Globalization of R&D Investment by US Multinational Enterprises: Evidence from Industry-Level Data. *International Journal of Economics and Finance, 8*(2), 51–69.

2

Strategic Choice of R&D FDI

Abstract From the received scholarly studies on R&D FDI, there are broadly two strategic motivations of R&D FDI. This includes home-based asset exploitation and home-based asset augmentation. While extant literatures are rich on the strategic choices of R&D FDIs, it's weak at offering detailed structure on the similarity and distinction between strategic and specific motivations of R&D FDI at the country level. This incomplete knowledge prompts a need to conceptualise the motivations of R&D FDI. This chapter aims to provide an extensive critical review of the extant literature on the strategic motivations of R&D FDI. The review of relevant literature will provide the theoretical background for the development of the study's conceptual framework and hypotheses.

Keywords Strategic • Exploitation • Augmentation • Internalisation • Internationalisation

O. Igbinigie et al., *Strategic Motivations of Inward R&D FDI*,
https://doi.org/10.1007/978-3-030-41015-5_2

Theories of MNE for Asset Exploitation

The motivations of FDI stem from several traditional theories of MNEs. These received theories of MNEs, in turn, could be extended to explain R&D FDI. It is interesting to note that R&D like other traditional elements of value-added activities of the firm (e.g. production) broadly shares the same motivations of traditional FDI (Criscuolo et al. 2005). Like traditional FDI, R&D investment would have its distinctive location factors, as well as each location responding with different factors (Demirbag et al. 2007; Nieto and Rodríguez 2011; Zheng 2011; Awate et al. 2015). Previous studies on this line of enquiry (like Cantwell and Piscitello 2002; Von Zedtwitz and Gassmann 2002; Cantwell and Mudambi 2000, 2005; Zheng 2011; Awate et al. 2015) have all shown that MNEs' R&D FDI follow twin strategies of asset exploitation or asset augmentation. These strategic motivations of MNEs' R&D FDI draw theoretical support from different traditional theories of MNEs.

From the received theories of MNEs, FDI occurs when MNE internationalises to exploit home-made firm-specific capabilities in foreign locations (Vernon 1966; Buckley and Casson 1976; Rugman 1981; Hennart 1982; Dunning 1988, 2001). Within this context, R&D FDI plays a pivotal role in exploiting pre-existing firm-specific capabilities in foreign locations (Ghoshal and Bartlett 1990; Vernon 1966). This perspective corroborates with studies that showed that MNEs establish manufacturing facilities abroad and co-locate R&D facilities to adapt existing products to local needs (Zheng 2011; Awate et al. 2015).

The earliest theoretical explanation that lends support to this perspective is the Hymer-Kindleberger hypothesis (Kindleberger 1969; Hymer 1976). According to Hymer-Kindleberger, FDI is about the international transfer of proprietary and intangible assets. Hymer (1960) proposed that MNEs possess firm-specific assets such as technology, business techniques, and skilled personnel; and that the market for the sales of these assets is imperfect. Hymer (1960) further argued that the existence of firm-specific advantage is essential for foreign firms to compete effectively in foreign markets given the fact that local firms have better knowledge of their locational economic environment than foreign firms. Kindleberger

(1969) added that imperfections in goods and factor markets coupled with government limitations influence the firm's choice to carry out FDI.

Following Hymer's theory, the product life cycle (PLC) theory also follows the market imperfection hypothesis (Vernon 1966, 1979). Vernon (1966, 1979) proposed that MNEs follow a gradual pace in their international trajectory usually from their immediate market where they acquire significant competences/specific assets over time, before investing in foreign markets. The PLC theory posits that the internationalisation process of the firm follows specific stages through the product life. The PLC theory emphasises the relevance of the home market considered as the preferred location for product innovation. Here, the home location is for product innovation considered as centre for product development. Although the PLC theory explicitly explained MNEs' behaviours in the location of foreign production abroad, issues concerning R&D in terms of either product and process innovation or the creation of knowledge are considered to remain at the home country, thus supporting home-based asset exploitation.

According to Vernon (1966) at the home country, the products are produced and exported to the international markets. However, the ability to export depends on the parent firm production advantage linked to its innovativeness and capabilities. As the product matures, the product enjoys lower production cost and more room to export. However, increase sales and profits call for increased competition from new entrants. Thus, brand differentiation and diversification will be the focus to protect market share. Production becomes concentrated in location with the least production costs to service the global market given the immense competition from rival firms. Here, less-developed countries become attractive as production locations due to potential cost-saving factors. In such case, the product can be exported back to the home market from the foreign production locations.

As a whole, PLC theory proposed that MNEs engage in foreign investment for exploitative purposes. The home market remains the centre for innovation and knowledge creation. This theoretical perspective can be extended to R&D activities by MNEs where R&D subsidiaries are co-located with foreign production to adapt products for foreign market demand. The applicability of PLC like other theories that fall within this strand of literature do not fully reflect with other FDI strategic motives of asset-seeking. One of the limitations of the PLC theory is that it mainly focused on developed MNEs investing in less-developed economies. Here, authors have argued that different economic conditions exist across different markets and as such MNEs may behave differently in other economic conditions outside that covered under PLC theory.

Another theory that tends to explain asset exploitation strategies of MNEs is the internalisation theory of MNEs initiated by Buckley and Casson (1976) and enriched by several other scholars like Rugman (1981), Hennart (1982), and Dunning (1988, 2001). This body of literature augments IB research by establishing the interaction between the external environment (market conditions) and the internal knowledge flows between MNEs and their foreign affiliates. Internalisation theorists proposed that market imperfections that exist in the intermediate product market may cause firm to incur high transaction cost or compromise the transfer of firm-specific knowledge to foreign markets (Petersen et al. 2010; Casson 2015).

The underlying assumption of internalisation theory like other industrial organisation-based theories of the firm like Hymer (1960), Kindleberger (1969), and Caves (1971) is that they recognised that MNEs possess home-made assets and that the cost associated with managing internalised market across borders is lower than those of external markets due to the existence of market imperfections. Buckley and Casson's (1976) economic analysis of the growth of MNEs showed that when markets for intermediate products are imperfect, there is internalisation advantage if firms bypass market imperfections by creating internal markets. By internalising foreign operations, a firm may gain significant control of its affiliates and therefore improve its ability to assure operational quality, avoid transaction and coordination costs, prevent leakage of valuable knowledge, and minimise the risk of property right infringements. Casson (2015) noted that internalising foreign activities could facilitate the implementation of strategies aimed at gaining certain benefits, such as discriminatory pricing and transfer pricing.

The internalisation theory of MNE has received its fair share of criticism from academic scholars. Some argued that internalisation theory is only valid in explaining high-tech and knowledge-intensive industries or

FDI flows from research-intensive economies such as the US to other fairly rich but less research-intensive countries, for example, in Western Europe, because their consumers could afford the sophisticated products generated by the new technologies (Tallman 2003). The generality of internalisation theory in explaining newly industrialising countries' "emerging market economies" such as China has not been fully accounted for (Casson 2015). Another criticism of internalisation theory has been a controversy with resource-based theorists. Critics contend that the emphasis of internalisation theory on ownership, property rights, and contracts distracts attention from the factors that are really important in explaining MNEs and FDI, which they maintain are primarily social, cultural, and organisational (Kogut and Zander 1992; Tallman 2003).

Building on the above theories, Dunning (1988, 1995) proposed an analytical framework by combining existing FDI theories to explain the patterns of MNEs' foreign activity known as the OLI framework. The OLI is an acronym that stands for Ownership, Location, and Internalisation; these represent three main sources of advantages synchronised by firms to motivate internationalisation expansion. Dunning (1988) argued that for a firm to compete successfully in foreign markets, such firm must possess ownership-specific advantages (OSAs) over its rival. The idea here is that MNEs possess firm-specific asset that is mobile but very unique (Dunning 1979). These assets can be applied to operations at different locations without reducing their effectiveness, for example, brand name, trademark, human technical know-how, managerial structure, product development, patents, marketing skills, and so on.

Dunning (1979) noted that the firm's OSA is a product of the national economic advantage of the firm's origin. Although OSA is unique to a firm, it is further augmented due to the multinationality of the firm's operations (Dunning 2006). This, therefore, suggests that today's OSA of a particular firm is yesterday's location advantage of the country of origin and experiences from multinationality of activities of the firm's operations. Adding to that, Dunning (1979, Dunning 2006) and Lundan (2010) showed that OSAs are in three distinctive groups; this includes ownership-asset advantages, economies of common governance, and institutional factors. The ownership-asset advantages relate to the innovative competence of the firm in terms of its intellectual property rights.

These assets are intangible and are rare to imitate (Lundan 2010). The second group is the economies of common governance created through the advantage of scale, while the third group relates to the aspect of the firm which incorporates firms' specific norms and values or corporate culture, codes of conduct, incentive systems, and an imprint of the institutional environment of the home country (see Dunning and Lundan 2008; Lundan 2010).

Location-specific advantage (LSA) components of the OLI framework are determined by the host country's comparative advantage, for example, the economic, physical, political, and psychic distance regarding the locational attractiveness to foreign investments. LSAs are considered to be immobile. However, firms' desire to invest in a particular location is partly inspired by transaction costs and by its desire to augment FSAs (Dunning 2009). The idea here is that location choice could be influenced by access to agglomeration externalities present in a centre of excellence other than natural endowment or cost-related factors. The competitiveness of a location could affect different types of MNE activity or types of FDI (Dunning 2009; Ali et al. 2010). Drawing from these perspectives, location choice decision is a consequence of a synergy of the foreign investment motives of the MNEs (OSAs) and what the location can offer (LSAs). However, how can the synergy between OSAs and LSAs be effectively exploited, should it be internalised or externalised?

The final component of the OLI framework specifically provides answers to the above question. The internalisation-specific advantage (ISA) is considered as the most important strand in the "three tripods" of Dunning's OLI framework. Traditionally, ISA elucidates how MNCs expand business globally overcoming market inefficiencies and effectively maximising net benefits of lower production and transaction costs (e.g. negotiation cost, default cost, moral hazard, adverse selection, protection from government, sustaining operational efficiency, control of market conditions, and protection of products' quality). From the original concept, the more a firm internalise its OSAs rather than externalise them, the more likely MNEs would be involved in foreign investments.

However, it is worth noting that the idea behind the original OLI framework has been considered to be static (Itaki 1991) and very much inclined on transaction cost approach (Brouthers et al. 1999; Dunning

2001). Adding to that, the operational practicality of OLI framework has also been questioned due to its many variables (the shopping list syndrome) (Dunning 2001). Parallel to this, rapid advancement in technology and globalisation activities of MNEs have impacted significantly on the ability of firms to transfer its OSAs across borders (with lower monitoring costs and increased strategic alliance) (Dunning 1995; Cantwell and Narula 2001). These perspectives have been considered in more recent writings in an effort to modify the framework to be more dynamic.

This perspective also corroborates with Dunning's view on asset augmentation and strategic alliance. According to Dunning, the collaboration between wealth-creating agents is no longer a symptom of structural market failure but rather as a means to jointly reduce endemic market failure (Dunning 1995, 2009). Dunning (2009) widens ISAs to capture not only the transaction cost perspective but also competitiveness enhancing goals of MNEs (via hierarchical and alliance capitalism). However, it is worth noting that hierarchical capitalism and alliance capitalism are not alternatives, but they are complementary to each other (Dunning 2006, 2009).

In light of the above, the applicability of the above theories does not fully reflect with other FDI strategic motives. This development has inspired large body of research, for instance, Cantwell et al. (2010) relying on path dependence, institutional environment, and evolutionary theory to examine the capabilities of firms and institutional systems (both internal and external). The study identified the scope for firm-level creativity and institutional entrepreneurship that may lead to co-evolution with the environment. Likewise, Teece (2014) developed a framework explaining how strategy and dynamic capabilities together determine firm-level sustained competitive advantage in global environments. It can be deduced, therefore, that a firm internalising or externalising depends on its prescient strategy linked with its capabilities towards enhancing global competitiveness rather than mere transaction cost consideration (also see Dunning and Zhang 2008).

Theories of MNE for Asset Augmentation

In contrast to the theories of MNEs' home-based asset exploitation motivations, some researchers have recently added that MNEs might be driven to augment the firms' knowledge base (Iwasa and Odagiri 2004; Lewin et al. 2009; Cantwell and Piscitello 2002; Cantwell and Mudambi 2000, 2005). This perspective corroborates with existing theories of MNEs that proposed that MNEs do not only transfer home-made knowledge but create knowledge or learn to create new knowledge in different international locations (Johanson and Vahlne 1977; Ghoshal and Bartlett 1990; Barney 1991; Kogut and Zander 1993; Rugman et al. 2011). These authors argued that each location has specific locational advantages for MNEs to facilitate knowledge creation or gain access to localised knowledge (Kuemmerle 1999; Cantwell and Piscitello 2002; Cantwell and Mudambi 2000, 2005).

The earliest IB theory that provide for learning in the international trajectory of MNEs is the Uppsala internationalisation model (Johanson and Wiedersheim-Paul 1975; Johanson and Vahlne 1977). As noted in Johanson and Wiedersheim-Paul (1975), the international trajectory of the firms follows a specific path where the firm first develops its business activities in the domestic market and then internationalises as a consequence of a series of incremental decisions backed by years of experiential learning. Johanson and Wiedersheim-Paul (1975) argued that before internationalisation, firms usually lack experience or the knowledge behind internationalisation strategies. As such, firms would enter foreign markets via sales agents through exporting. Overtime, firms would replace sales agents with sales subsidiaries and later go into production as the level of its knowledge increases. This knowledge can only be acquired over time through incremental decision-making, learning, and experience about foreign market and operations (Johanson and Vahlne 1977). This, therefore, suggests that the more the firm gains knowledge in foreign operations, the more its commitment via foreign investments (Johanson and Vahlne 1977).

The risk and uncertainty MNEs experience in foreign markets occur due to differences in geographical/psychic distance. Johanson and Vahlne

(1977) described psychic distance as the sum of factors preventing the flow of information from, or to, the market; these could be differences in economic, political, social, and cultural systems. Johanson and Vahlne (1977) identified two interdependent criterions that determine the internationalisation process of the firm; these include experiential learning and commitment building. They further added trust-building, opportunity identification, and knowledge accumulation as part of firms' experiential learning curve which directly influences firms' level of commitment in foreign market (Johanson and Vahlne 2003, 2009). Although, the Uppsala internationalisation model established the relevance of experience and learning in building competence and capability towards internationalisation, however, the model had been criticised for its emphasis on risk avoidance and that it had limitations on two fronts: first is the weakness in explaining the rapid internationalisation of certain firms, like born global MNEs (Oviatt and McDougall 1994, 2000). Second, the model does not explain how knowledge gained in one location can be helpful in another location.

Building on the Uppsala internationalisation model of MNEs, evolutionary theorists theorised how unfolding economic events over time shapes organisational learning, survival, and development (Nelson 2002; Nelson and Winter 2009). Evolutionary theorists proposed that evolutionary trajectory of MNEs is an outcome of years of experiential learning and development. Unlike the Uppsala model that emphasised market imperfections, the evolutionary trajectory of MNEs disregards the relevance of market imperfection (in terms of opportunism) in explaining the evolutionary internalisation of MNEs (Kogut and Zander 1993). Kogut and Zander (1993) perceived MNE, not as an institution focused on mitigating market imperfections, but as having a "combinative capability" beyond the reach of alternative technology transfer modes. Kogut and Zander (1993) argued that MNEs possess combinative capability which reflects prior accumulated knowledge (embedded in operational routine), and the tacit nature of its knowledge determines the future development strategy of the MNEs.

Kogut and Zander (1993) further argued that the tacitness (complexity) of knowledge, the more firms internalise. That is, knowledge that is difficult to codify is internalised and is resistant to rapid imitation. Here,

MNEs are recognised as one of the most efficient and effective channels to transfer knowledge. This position has drawn some attention from other authors to debunk Kogut and Zaheer's (1993 findings by re-examining their empirical results to conclude that market imperfection and transaction cost theory remain crucial to MNEs' international expansion (Love 1995; McFetridge 1995). Verbeke (2003) concluded that Kogut and Zaheer's (1993) evolutionary model of MNEs is an enriched internalisation perspective or learning perspective. Verbeke (2003) proposed that both models are useful building blocks in a perhaps more eclectic analytical framework. Such eclectic framework is likely to permit the joint study of co-evolving organisational routines (which can be used to define the MNE's broader governance structure) and technological competences. The evolutionary model of MNEs thus provided a crude perspective of how MNEs accumulate knowledge and capabilities over time; the model had been criticised on its failure to explain how multi-subsidiaries by MNEs in foreign locations complement each other towards overall competitiveness of the firm (Buckley 2009; Rugman et al. 2011).

In the light of the above, some IB scholars have incorporated the international networking model in the study of MNEs' behaviour (e.g. Ghoshal and Bartlett 1990; Tsai 2002; Buckley 2009; Rugman et al. 2011; Zaheer and Nachum 2011; Regner and Zander 2011; Fang et al. 2013). These authors argued that MNEs forge linkage with foreign networks by establishing a presence in foreign countries, to enhance its competitiveness. Here, MNEs are presented as a complex integrated network with dispersed (external) and concentrated (internal) knowledge systems. MNEs by virtue of their global scope and strategy can derive further advantage from their ability to tap into global and local networks of knowledge. Knowledge from various sources and locations leads to strong competitive advantage. Within the IB literature, the assertion is that firm-specific advantages (FSAs) enable firms to engage in FDI and overcome liabilities of foreignness (Zaheer 1995; Rugman 2005; Rugman and Collinson 2012). Under the purview of the network theory, authors argued that network resources provide idiosyncratic and inimitable resources which facilitate internationalisation of firms' circumventing market entry barriers and risks of FDI (Zaheer et al. 2000; Chen 2003;

Giroud and Scott-Kennel 2009; Asmussen et al. 2013). According to Jean et al. (2011), a firm's position in their home country's network determines its ability to mobilise resources within the network for international endeavours. This goes to show that FDI via network linkage may be initiated by one firm but may entail actions by other members in the network.

Jean et al. (2011) and Holm et al. (1996) noted that dominant members in the network can orchestrate concerted actions among its members to penetrate foreign market or to establish production plants in a foreign location. This perspective corroborates with Johanson and Vahlne (2009) assertion that a firm that does not have a position in a relevant international business network subjects itself to liabilities of outsidership and foreignness. Chen (2003) revealed that small and weak Taiwanese firms propel the process of internationalisation by making maximum use of external network to which they have access. Chen (2003) added that firms exploit external resources, as opposed to firm-specific assets. Here, FDI takes place if firms can leverage external resources, but the leverage will be successful only if the network relations are competently managed by the investor. The successful leverage of external resources increases the power of the investor, whose position in the network improves (with more FDIs), which in turn enables the investor to increase its leverage. According to Holm et al. (1996), FDI does not only serve as conduit to maintain network relationship but also to change relationships in favour of the investor. As argued by Madhavan et al. (1998), the struggle for position in the network is the main driving force for network evolution.

Some other studies have shown that business networks are driven by social factors such as ethnic ties, rather than economic factors. For example, Zaheer et al. (2009) revealed that ethnic networks exert greater influence than cluster capabilities on location decisions of FDI in services to India. Jean et al. (2011) revealed that networks through ethnic ties impact on FDI location choice and firm's performance. In another related study, authors have shown that social networks such as Japanese *Keiretsu* and Chinese *Guanxi* played a crucial role in doing business in China or Japan (Buckley et al. 2006; Lee et al. 2001). These authors attributed the rise in ethnic networks to lack of sufficient institutional support, particularly in emerging markets. As stated by Chen and Chen (1998), the network becomes relevant in a foreign location with weak institutional infrastructure, for example, China, but becomes less important for entering mature market like the US due to the quality of institutional infrastructure. These findings also corroborate with Jean et al.'s (2011) assertion that, coupled with strong network links, firm also needs to have firm-specific assets to be successful in foreign markets. Adding to that, Bell (1995) and Coviello and Munro (1995) also noted that strong network links might also inhabit the innovativeness of a firm by limiting their choice of foreign market and entry mode. Also, Cantwell (2009) argued that the tendency of local networks hindering firms' innovativeness might also result in adverse selection in favour of laggards over leaders in knowledge-intensive industry. From the preceding text, network theory can be said to explain MNEs' international behaviour engaging in FDI between or within emerging markets. The network theory becomes limited in explaining MNEs' FDI between developed economies and emerging markets.

Mathews (2006) developed the linkage, leverage, and learning(LLL) theory to proffer another theoretical perspective on how MNEs from emerging markets carry out FDI in developed markets. According to Mathews (2006), EM MNEs tap into the global market place based on three interrelated strategies. First, they link up with firms around the globe. Second, they leverage such links to overcome resource barriers (e.g. joint venture or partnership). Third, they learn to build up their capabilities in a cumulative fashion. These three strategic drivers by linkage, leverage, and learning are what makes emerging MNEs' international expansion different compared with MNEs from advanced economies. Behind this theoretical perspective is the rise of East Asian countries starting from Japan, Hong Kong, China, and Singapore (World Bank 1993). These countries incubate MNEs that are now major players in the global market place. In other words, these latecomers in the global market place have been able to exploit their late arrival to tap into advanced technologies and accelerate their uptake and learning efforts utilising various forms of collaborative processes and state assistance to compete within the global market (Mathews 2006; Dunning 2006), encapsulated by three classic objectives including the catch-up goal, imitation, and learning (Mathews 2006).

The linkage notion to globalisation by EM MNEs focuses on the goal of the MNEs. There are three distinctive features to linkage strategy. First, unlike MNEs from advanced economies that exploit or augment existing assets in international market place, EM MNEs gain access to resources through their international expansion (Peng 2001). Second, MNEs from advanced economies see the world as full of competitors who are trying to imitate their success, while the emerging markets' newcomers and latecomers see the world as full of resources to be tapped, provided the appropriate complementary strategies and organisational forms can be devised. Third, EM MNEs' outward orientation carries higher risk and uncertainties than a more conservative inward focus conventional MNEs from advanced economies. Thus, EM MNEs device strategies overcoming problems of market intelligence and knowledge in the foreign market by engaging in partnership or joint venture or any form of alliance. Put differently, EM MNEs adopt the easiest and secure mode of entry into foreign market to gain knowledge and resources and expand market share.

The leverage strategy to globalisation by EM MNEs focuses on how such linkage can be established with partners so that resources can be leveraged, that is, the imitability or transferability of the resources and their leverage potentials. By contrast, drawing from the stage theory perspective, firms develop internal resources (ownership) to exploit external opportunities and then internalise such resources for economic gains. In contrast, with Mathew's linkage, leverage, and learning strategy, MNEs scan the global market (goal) for resources that can be substituted or imitated (i.e. no ownership) to exploit external opportunities. Alignment or leverage potential then focuses on ways firms could secure such resources in the foreign market. In other words, repeated alignment with foreign firms should result in learning to develop knowledge and, then, hypothetically gain ownership of resources to exploit opportunities.

However, if traditional firms build their FSAs gradually (stage theory) and then internationalise in locations that help sustain or develop its FSAs, then does the appearance of EM MNEs in global market place anyway different from the internationalisation strategy of MNEs from advanced economies? Answer to this question can be likened to the thoughts in Cantwell and Narula (2001) that MNEs will not always partner with leaders. The idea here is that in a dynamic environment there is a possibility of technological change by having ties with a wide network of companies including those firms that have yet to demonstrate competence in the global arena could represent a higher learning potential for all partners. Alliance provides an opportunity to examine the nature of partner's competencies ultimately resulting in exploitation or augmentation. In light of this, it seems natural for MNEs especially from EM to invest in more advanced countries to access and augment as well as exploit their ownership advantages (Narula 2006).

As noted in Narula (2006) and Dunning (2006), some EM MNEs still possess a certain level of FSAs either from ownership or from geographical advantages, which should propel their internationalisation expansion. Even the ability to manage and coordinate intra-firm and interfirm transactions is central to the firm's competitiveness. Dunning (2006) reiterated that EM MNEs' success and failure in adding to their ownership advantages in a particular time is influenced by the location choice and mode of entry. In conclusion, the LLL framework provides insight into how EM MNEs build their advantages in the global market arena. However, the framework seems to be tailored to explain foreign investments between EM MNEs investing in advanced economies and totally ignored foreign investments that may occur between EM MNEs. Also, the role of institutions in EM MNEs' globalisation phenomena was not accounted for in the linkage, leverage, and learning framework.

Another emerging theory from the LLL framework is the springboard model developed by Luo and Tung (2007), Bonaglia et al. (2007), Luo and Wang (2012), and Madhok and Keyhani (2012). These authors demonstrate how EM firms bypass stringent foreign market trade barriers (liabilities of newness) with secured home government preferential treatment and incentives, to exploit their newly gained competitive advantages in other emerging or developing markets. Here, emerging markets' (EM) MNEs outward foreign investments portray an opportunity to accumulate strategic assets to compensate for competitive disadvantages due to the home market's institutions and market deficiencies.

Traditionally, EMs are expected to import capital, including FDI, and not export them until years of inward FDI before becoming prosperous and competitive enough to produce their own MNEs (Dunning 1988). Thus, the emergence of MNEs from developing countries poses interesting puzzles for extant theories of MNEs particularly about how MNEs are born, where, and why and modes of internationalisation. One of the bedrocks of international business theory is that MNEs are born in developed countries where home-made self-created assets or ownership advantages are incubated, nurtured, and exported abroad. Thus, finding EMs producing MNEs given their lack of economic and technological capabilities to inspire self-created assets still puzzles academic scholars. The mystery here is what types of OSAs inspire EM MNEs' foreign activities (if any) and at what degree such OSAs can inspire multinational activities and its sustainability.

In the literature, there are basically three extreme views as to developing new theories explaining the behaviour of EM MNEs' foreign activities. On the one hand, some authors argued that EM MNEs are a new species of multinationals that should be explained by new theories (Mathews 2006; Luo and Tung 2007), while some authors support the argument for new thinking to modify extant theories without developing new ones (Dunning 2006; Dunning et al. 2008). Others argued that existing theories are adequate and fully explain EM multinationals, thus no need to rethink conventional theories or to develop new theories (Narula 2006; Lessard and Lucea 2008; Rugman 2010).

Dunning (2006) acknowledged the need for new thinking about emerging economy MNEs recognising their lack of traditional OSAs. However, as persuasively shown in Dunning et al. (2008), changes between the pre-globalisation period and the post-globalisation period evidence by increased economic liberalisation in many emerging markets and advance markets, coupled with novel technological advancements, accelerated investment development path for EM MNEs. However, Dunning et al. (2008) reaffirmed the validity of the OLI framework to fully explain the existence of EM MNEs despite their lack of self-created assets but heavy reliance on country-specific advantages (CSAs).

Narula (2006), Lessard and Lucea (2008), and Rugman (2010) adopt a more radical approach that EM MNEs do not have firm-specific advantages (FSAs) besides economies of scale and privileged access to country-specific advantage (CSA) evidence by low-cost labour, cheap finance, and natural resources. These CSAs are available to all firms and cannot provide long-term or sustainable multinational activity. Unlike CSAs, self-created assets or FSAs are the source of extraordinary rent, for instance, cutting-edge technology and strong brand. Their position is that firm-specific advantage and country-specific advantage model of internationalisation fully explains the behaviour of EM MNEs. As such, there is no need for new theories as there is lack of sustainable investments by EM multinationals. Hence, new theories will have to wait until EM MNEs accumulate real FSAs. As reiterated in Rugman (2010), the weak form of FSA currently possessed by EM MNEs tends to be confined to intra-regional operations rather than the perceived global reach in Friedman (2006).

Within the academic literature, the consensus is that EM MNEs expand abroad without OSAs ex ante. This perspective has drawn support from several scholars (Mathews 2006; Luo and Tung 2007; Ramamurti 2012). According to these authors, EM multinationals are a new species of MNEs that should be explained by new theories. The idea is that the inconsistency of traditional theories of MNEs regarding internationalisation trajectories of EM MNEs and advance market (AM) MNEs is reflected in differences in their OLI advantages. A core tenet of Dunning's OLI model is that exploitation of OSAs abroad is efficiently done in synergy with targeted host LSAs and internalisation advantages due to market imperfections. The assumption here is the OSAs are unique to a firm, LSAs are freely available to all firms including foreign firms, while internalisation advantage is largely influenced by market imperfections and profit maximisation objectives. However, emerging economy MNE theorists assert that EM MNEs possess a special kind of OSAs that are suitable for other emerging markets (Ramamurti 2012; Cuervo-Cazurra 2011, 2012). Even that, LSAs are not freely available to all firms (Hennart 2012), plus EM MNEs internationalise differently with risk-riveting behaviour (Mathews 2006; Govindarajan and Ramamurti 2011; Ramamurti 2012; Madhok and Keyhani 2012).

In light of the above, authors argued that emerging economies tend to be characterised by the lower level of income per capita; this may induce firms to generate less sophisticated innovations that are appropriate for low-income consumers (Prahalad 2008; Cuervo-Cazurra 2011, 2012). As noted in Ramamurti (2012), EM MNEs possess self-created assets more suitable to other emerging markets, for instance, the ability to operate in difficult business environment and the ability to produce products at ultralow costs and with the right features to meet consumers' needs. Similarly, Govindarajan and Ramamurti (2011) noted that EM MNEs do create innovations with great market potentials even in rich countries (known in the literature as reverse innovation). Although EM MNEs apply novel and innovative combinations of existing knowledge and technologies, such innovations tend not to involve technological breakthroughs of the kind that drive innovation in developed countries (Govindarajan and Ramamurti 2011).

Adding to that, Hennart (2012) argued that if FSAs are internalised abroad due to market imperfections as such markets for complimentary local assets are equally subject to imperfections. In that, EM MNEs have preferential access over subsets of CSAs at home to generate the profits needed to acquire FSAs they lack to compete with foreign MNEs first at home and then abroad (see Smith 2007; Williamson and Zeng 2009). For example, restriction imposes on foreign ownership of local distribution assets (Sull and Wang 2013) or state ownership of mineral deposits and lands. This monopoly power can often be used to benefit local firms in detriment to foreign firms. A phenomenon Vernon (1979) called the *obsolescing bargain*. This may result to a bundling effect where foreign MNEs are faced with the choice between fully owned MNE affiliates (if allowed) and joint ventures with local firms depending on the transactional properties of the complimentary local resources held by local owners as well as the transactional properties of the intangibles held by foreign MNEs. More so, there is also a general consensus among observers that markets for technology are becoming more competitive, lowering the bargaining power of technology developers (see Williamson and Zeng 2009). As persuasively shown in Kumaraswamy et al. (2012), catching up does not necessarily require the broad and deep knowledge base to innovate. Imitators can readily leapfrog to new technologies; unlike their established rivals, they do not have sunk investments in old technologies. From this perspective it is deducible that having self-created assets exploitable abroad is not sufficient to guarantee success if the needed local complimentary resources cannot be efficiently accessed.

Another puzzling perspective in the differences in internationalisation trajectories of EM MNEs and AM MNEs is related to predictions by stage theory of MNEs. Following the predictions of stage model of internationalisation (Johanson and Vahlne 1977, 2003), the assumption is that firms expand to countries similar to their home country before expanding to other dissimilar countries and only increase its commitments in host country incrementally if things go well. Adding to that, following the product life cycle hypothesis (Vernon 1979), FDIs should flow from developed countries to less-developed countries and not the other way around. However, EM MNEs appear to violate some core tenets of stage approach to internationalisation as noted in Ramamurti (2004), Govindarajan and Ramamurti (2011), Ramamurti (2012), and Madhok and Keyhani (2012); these authors argued that EM MNEs internationalise at a much faster pace than the stage model predicts, targeting host countries that are considered physically or economically distant before expanding into more proximate and similar countries. Drawing from Ghoshal and Bartlett (2000) and Madhok and Keyhani (2012), EM MNEs build on their resources and capabilities they already possess as they internationalise regardless of whether they are currently valuable or not.

The increased foreign activities by EM MNEs from South to North than from South to South and propensity to use high-commitment foreign entry strategies, for instance, merger and acquisition, rather than other more conservative and low-risk foreign entry strategies such as use of sales agent or sales subsidiaries (Ramamurti 2012; Madhok and Keyhani 2012) have also puzzled scholars. As revealed in Yiu et al. (2007), Cuervo-Cazurra and Genc (2008), and Cuervo-Cazurra (2012), EM MNEs' risk-riveting behaviour is deeply rooted in their poorly developed institutions, for instance, less stable political systems and weak law enforcement which may induce firms to develop the ability to effectively manage high transaction costs in an unstable environment. Alternatively, EM MNEs may tend to escape home markets' institutional constraints by entering countries with better institutions and stringent governance. This viewpoint draws support from the argument in Bonaglia et al. (2007) and Williamson and Zeng (2009), deducing that the world has become flatter and that changes in global business environment significantly lower the cost and risk of internationalisation, thus inducing EM MNEs to catch up quickly with developed countries' MNEs.

In summary, it is reasonable to suggest that EM MNEs expand abroad to developed countries to exploit the difference in dissimilarities rather than similarities. This may be to gain access to market with consumers with high income per capita or to obtain advanced technologies through acquisitions of established industries in developed countries. Adding to that, beyond the institutional support and complementary locational assets that shape the behaviour of EM multinationals, EM theory failed to explain the international entrepreneurship of this breed of multinational firms. This may perhaps explain why their lack of OSAs is cushion with strong managerial and organisational prowess.

Conclusion

This chapter provides an extensive review of the extant literature on the strategic and specific motivations of R&D FDI. From this, it has been observed that MNEs play a pivotal role in the generation of technology and its transmission across locations, which in turn help to exploit or augment the competitive advantage of the MNE. The heterogeneity of a firm's specific capabilities allows MNEs to invest in foreign markets and achieve a competitive advantage. MNE R&D subsidiaries international trajectories will thus depend on the technological capability of the parent firm, hence providing theoretical support for R&D FDI to follow different strategies and specific motivations. The next chapter provides a review of the empirical literature on locational factors of FDI and R&D FDI.

References

Ali, F. A., Fiess, N., & MacDonald, R. (2010). Do institutions matter for foreign direct investment? *Open Economies Review, 21*(2), 201–219.

Asmussen, C. G., Foss, N. J., & Pedersen, T. (2013). Knowledge transfer and accommodation effects in multinational corporations evidence from European subsidiaries. *Journal of Management, 39*(6), 1397–1429.

Awate, S., Larsen, M. M., & Mudambi, R. (2015). Accessing vs sourcing knowledge: A comparative study of R&D internationalization between emerging and advanced economy firms. *Journal of International Business Studies, 46*(1), 63–86.
Barney, J. (1991). Firm resources and sustained competitive advantage. *Journal of Management, 17*(1), 99–120.
Bell, J. (1995). The internationalization of small computer software firms: A further challenge to "stage" theories. *European Journal of Marketing, 29*(8), 60–75.
Bonaglia, F., Goldstein, A., & Mathews, J. A. (2007). Accelerated internationalization by emerging markets' multinationals: The case of the white goods sector. *Journal of World Business, 42*(4), 369–383.
Brouthers, L.E., Brouthers, K.D., & Werner, S. (1999). Is Dunning's eclectic framework descriptive or normative? *Journal of International Business Studies, 30*(4), 831–844.
Buckley, P. J. (2009). Internalisation thinking: From the multinational enterprise to the global factory. *International Business Review, 18*(3), 224–235.
Buckley, P. J., & Casson, M. (1976). *The future of the multinational enterprise*. London: Macmillan.
Buckley, P.J., Clegg, J., & Tan, H. (2006). Cultural awareness in knowledge transfer to China—The role of guanxi and mianzi. *Journal of World Business, 41*(3), 275–288.
Cantwell, J. (2009). Location and the multinational enterprise. *Journal of International Business Studies, 40*(1), 35–41.
Cantwell, J., & Mudambi, R. (2000). The location of MNE R&D Activity: The role of investment incentives. *MIR: Management International Review, 40*(1), 127–148.
Cantwell, J., & Mudambi, R. (2005). MNE competence-creating subsidiary mandates. *Strategic Management Journal, 26*(12), 1109–1128.
Cantwell, J., & Narula, R. (2001). The eclectic paradigm in the global economy. *International Journal of the Economics of Business, 8*(2), 155–172.
Cantwell, J., & Piscitello, L. (2002). The location of technological activities of MNCs in European regions: The role of spillovers and local competencies. *Journal of International Management, 8*(1), 69–96.
Cantwell, J., Dunning, J. H., & Lundan, S. M. (2010). An evolutionary approach to understanding international business activity: The co-evolution of MNEs and the institutional environment. *Journal of International Business Studies, 41*(4), 567–586.

Casson, M. (2015). Coase and international business: The origin and development of internalization theory. *Managerial and Decision Economics, 36*(1), 55–66.

Caves, R. E. (1971). International corporations: The industrial economics of foreign investment. *Economica, 88*(149), 1–27.

Chen, T. (2003). Network resources for internationalization: The case of Taiwan's electronics firms. *Journal of Management Studies, 40*(5), 1107–1130.

Chen, H., & Chen, T. (1998). Network linkages and location choice in foreign direct investment. *Journal of International Business Studies, 29*(3), 445–467.

Coviello, N. E., & Munro, H. J. (1995). Growing the entrepreneurial firm: Networking for international market development. *European Journal of Marketing, 29*(7), 49–61.

Criscuolo, P., Narula, R., & Verspagen, B. (2005). Role of home and host country innovation systems in R&D internationalisation: A patent citation analysis. *Economics of Innovation and New Technology, 14*(5), 417–433.

Cuervo-Cazurra, A. (2011). Global strategy and global business environment: The direct and indirect influences of the home country on a firm's global strategy. *Global Strategy Journal, 1*(3–4), 382–386.

Cuervo-Cazurra, A. (2012). Extending theory by analyzing developing country multinational companies: Solving the goldilocks debate. *Global Strategy Journal, 2*(3), 153–167.

Cuervo-Cazurra, A., & Genc, M. (2008). Transforming Disadvantages into Advantages: Developing-Country MNEs in the Least Developed Countries. *Journal of International Business Studies, 39*(6), 957–979.

Demirbag, M., Tatoglu, E., & Glaister, K. W. (2007). Dimensions of European direct investment activity in Turkey: Patterns and prospects. *International Journal of Emerging Markets, 2*(3), 274–297.

Dunning, J. H. (1979). Explaining Changing Patterns of International Production: In Defence of the Eclectic Theory: Explaining Changing Patterns of International Production. *Oxford Bulletin of Economics and Statistics, 41*(4), pp. 269–295.

Dunning, J. H. (1988). The eclectic paradigm of international production: A restatement and some possible extensions. *Journal of International Business Studies, 4*(7), 1–31.

Dunning, J. H. (1995). Reappraising the eclectic paradigm in an age of alliance capitalism. *Journal of International Business Studies, 6*(12), 461–491.

Dunning, J. H. (2001). The eclectic (OLI) paradigm of international production: Past, present and future. *International Journal of the Economics of Business, 8*(2), 173–190.

Dunning, J. H. (2006). Comment on dragon multinationals: New players in 21st century globalization. *Asia Pacific Journal of Management, 23*(2), 139–141.

Dunning, J. H. (2009). Location and the multinational enterprise: John Dunning's thoughts on receiving the journal of international business studies 2008 decade award. *Journal of International Business Studies, 40*(1), 20–34.

Dunning, J. H., & Lundan, S. M. (2008). Institutions and the OLI paradigm of the multinational enterprise. *Asia Pacific Journal of Management, 25*(4), 573–593.

Dunning, J. H., Kim, C., & Park, D. (2008). Old wine in new bottles: A comparison of emerging-market TNCs today and developed-country TNCs thirty years ago. *University of Oxford, working paper,* no. 011.

Dunning, J. H., & Zhang, F. (2008). Foreign direct investment and the locational competitiveness of countries. *Transnational Corporations, 17*(3), 1.

Fang, Y., Wade, M., Delios, A., & Beamish, P. W. (2013). An exploration of multinational enterprise knowledge resources and foreign subsidiary performance. *Journal of World Business, 48*(1), 30–38.

Friedman, T. L. (2006). *The world is flat [updated and expanded]: A brief history of the twenty-first century*. London: Palgrave Macmillan

Ghoshal, S., & Bartlett, C. A. (1990). The multinational corporation as an interorganizational network. *Academy of Management Review, 15*(4), 603–626.

Ghoshal, S. & Bartlett, C. A., (2000). *Going global: lessons from late movers.* Massachusetts: Harvard Business School Press.

Giroud, A., & Scott-Kennel, J. (2009). MNE linkages in international business: A framework for analysis. *International Business Review, 18*(6), 555–566.

Govindarajan, V., & Ramamurti, R. (2011). Reverse innovation, emerging markets, and global strategy. *Global Strategy Journal, 1*(3–4), 191–205.

Hennart, J. (1982). *A theory of multinational enterprise.* Michigan: University of Michigan Press.

Hennart, J. (2012). Emerging market multinationals and the theory of the multinational enterprise. *Global Strategy Journal, 2*(3), 168–187.

Holm, D. B., Eriksson, K., & Johanson, J. (1996). Business networks and cooperation in international business relationships. *Journal of International Business Studies, 27*(5), 1033–1053.

Hymer, S. (1960). *On multinational corporations and foreign direct investment. The theory of transnational corporations.* London: Routledge for the United Nations.

Hymer, S. H. (1976). *The international operations of national firms: A study of direct foreign investment.* MA: MIT Press Cambridge.

Itaki, M. (1991). A critical assessment of the eclectic theory of the multinational enterprise. *Journal of International Business Studies, 22*(3), 445–460.

Iwasa, T., & Odagiri, H. (2004). Overseas R&D, knowledge sourcing, and patenting: An empirical study of Japanese R&D investment in the US. *Research Policy, 33*(5), 807–828.

Jean, R. B., Tan, D., & Sinkovics, R. R. (2011). Ethnic ties, location choice, and firm performance in foreign direct investment: A study of Taiwanese business groups FDI in China. *International Business Review, 20*(6), 627–635.

Johanson, J., & Vahlne, J. (1977). The internationalization process of the firm-a model of knowledge development and increasing foreign market commitments. *Journal of International Business Studies, 2*(7), 23–32.

Johanson, J., & Vahlne, J. E. (2003). Business relationship learning and commitment in the internationalization process. *Journal of International Entrepreneurship, 1*(1), 83–101.

Johanson, J., & Vahlne, J. E. (2009). The Uppsala internationalization process model revisited: From liability of foreignness to liability of outsidership. *Journal of international business studies, 40*(9), 1411–1431.

Johanson, J, & Wiedersheim-Paul, F. (1975). The internationalization of the firm: Four Swedish cases, *Journal of Management Studies, 12*(3), 305–322.

Kindleberger, C. P. (1969). American business abroad. *Thunderbird International Business Review, 11*(2), 11–12.

Kogut, B., & Zander, U. (1992). Knowledge of the firm, combinative capabilities, and the replication of technology. *Organization Science, 3*(3), 383–397.

Kogut, B. and Zander, U. (1993). Knowledge of the firm and the evolutionary theory of the multinational corporation. *Journal of International Business Studies, 24*(4), 625–645.

Kuemmerle, W. (1999). Foreign direct investment in industrial research in the pharmaceutical and electronics industries-results from a survey of multinational firms. *Research Policy, 28*(2), 179–193.

Kumaraswamy, A., Mudambi, R., Saranga, H., & Tripathy, A. (2012). Catch-up strategies in the Indian auto components industry: Domestic firms' responses to market liberalization. *Journal of International Business Studies, 43*(4), 368–395.

Lee, D., Pae, J. H., & Wong, Y. (2001). A model of close business relationships in China (guanxi). *European Journal of Marketing, 35*(1/2), 51–69.

Lessard, D. R., & Lucea, R. (2008). Mexican multinationals. In R. Ramamurti & J. V. Singh (Eds.), *Emerging multinationals from emerging markets* (pp. 56–74). Cambridge: Cambridge University Press.

Lewin, A.Y., Massini, S. and Peeters, C. (2009). Why are companies offshoring innovation? The emerging global race for talent. *Journal of International Business Studies, 40*(6), 901–925.
Love, J. H. (1995). Knowledge, market failure and the multinational enterprise: A theoretical note. *Journal of International Business Studies, 26*(2), 399–407.
Lundan, S. M. (2010). What are ownership advantages? *Multinational Business Review, 18*(2), 51–70.
Luo, Y., & Tung, R. L. (2007). International expansion of emerging market enterprises: A springboard perspective. *Journal of International Business Studies, 38*(4), 481–498.
Luo, Y., & Wang, S. L. (2012). Foreign direct investment strategies by developing country multinationals: A diagnostic model for home country effects. *Global Strategy Journal, 2*(3), 244–261.
Madhavan, R., Koka, B. R., & Prescott, J. E. (1998). Networks in transition: How industry events(re) shape interfirm relationships. *Strategic Management Journal, 19*(5), 439–459.
Madhok, A., & Keyhani, M. (2012). Acquisitions as entrepreneurship: Asymmetries, opportunities, and the internationalization of multinationals from emerging economies. *Global Strategy Journal, 2*(1), 26–40.
Mathews, J. A. (2006). Dragon multinationals: New players in 21st century globalization. *Asia Pacific Journal of Management, 23*(1), 5–27.
McFetridge, D. G. (1995). Knowledge, market failure and the multinational enterprise: A comment. *Journal of International Business Studies, 4*(2), 409–415.
Narula, R. (2006). Globalization, new ecologies, new zoologies, and the purported death of the eclectic paradigm. *Asia Pacific Journal of Management, 23*(2), 143–151.
Nelson, R. R. (2002). Bringing institutions into evolutionary growth theory. *Journal of Evolutionary Economics, 12*(1–2), 17–28.
Nelson, R. R., & Winter, S. G. (2009). *An evolutionary theory of economic change*. Cambridge: Harvard University Press.
Nieto, M. J., & Rodríguez, A. (2011). Offshoring of R&D: Looking abroad to improve innovation performance. *Journal of International Business Studies, 42*(3), 345–361.
Oviatt, B. M., & McDougall, P. P. (1994). Toward a Theory of International New Ventures, *Journal of International Business Studies, 25*(1), 45–64.
Oviatt, B. M., & McDougall, P. P. (2000). International Entrepreneurship: The Intersection of Two Research Paths. *Academy of Management Journal, 43*(5), 902–906.

Peng, M. W. (2001). The resource-based view and international business. *Journal of Management, 27*(6), 803–829.
Petersen, B., Welch, L. S., & Benito, G. R. (2010). Managing the internalisation process. *Management International Review, 50*(2), 137–154.
Prahalad, C. (2008). The fortune at the bottom of the pyramid: Eradicating poverty through profits. *McKinsey briefing notes series, 36*(3), 52–74.
Ramamurti, R. (2004). Developing countries and MNEs: Extending and enriching the research agenda. *Journal of International Business Studies, 35*(4), 277–283.
Ramamurti, R. (2012). What is really different about emerging market multinationals? *Global Strategy Journal, 2*(1), 41–47.
Regner, P., & Zander, U. (2011). Knowledge and strategy creation in multinational companies. *Management International Review, 51*(6), 821–850.
Rugman, A. M. (1981). A test of internalization theory. *Managerial and Decision Economics, 2*(4), 211–219.
Rugman, A. M. (2005). *The regional multinationals: MNEs and global strategic management*. Cambridge: Cambridge University Press.
Rugman, A.M. (2010). *Do we need a new theory to explain emerging market multinationals. Foreign Direct Investment from Emerging Markets: The Challenges Ahead*. New York: Palgrave McMillan.
Rugman, A. M., & Collinson, S. (2012). *International business* (6th ed.). New Jersey: Pearson Prentice Hall.
Rugman, A. M., Verbeke, A., Nguyen, C., & Quyen, T. K. (2011). Fifty years of international business theory and beyond. *Management International Review, 51*(6), 755–786.
Smith, R. (2007). Dragons at your door: How Chinese cost innovation is disrupting global competition. *Research-Technology Management, 50*(5), 70.
Sull, D. N., & Wang, Y. (2013). *Made in China: What western managers can learn from trailblazing Chinese entrepreneurs*. Cambridge: Harvard Business Press.
Tallman, S. (2003). The significance of Bruce Kogut's and Udo Zander's article, 'Knowledge of the firm and the evolutionary theory of the multinational corporation'. *Journal of International Business Studies, 34*(6), 495–497.
Teece, D. J. (2014). A dynamic capabilities-based entrepreneurial theory of the multinational enterprise. *Journal of International Business Studies, 45*(1), 8–37.
Tsai, W. (2002). Social structure of "coopetition" within a multiunit organization: Coordination, competition, and intraorganizational knowledge sharing. *Organization Science, 13*(2), 179–190.

Verbeke, A. (2003). The evolutionary view of the MNE and the future of internalization theory. *Journal of International Business Studies, 34*(6), 498–504.
Vernon, R. (1966). International investment and international trade in the product cycle. *Quarterly Journal of Economics, 80*(2), 190–207.
Vernon, R. (1979). The product cycle hypothesis in new international environment. *Oxford Bulletin of Economics and Statistics, 41*(4), 255–267.
Von Zedtwitz, M., & Gassmann, O. (2002). Market versus technology drive in R&D internationalization: Four different patterns of managing research and development. *Research Policy, 31*(4), 569–588.
Williamson, P. J., & Zeng, M. (2009). Value-for-money strategies for recessionary times. *Harvard Business Review, 87*(3), 66–74.
World Bank. (1993). *The east Asian miracle*. New York: Oxford University Press.
Yiu, D. W., Lu, Y., Bruton, G. D., & Hoskisson, R. E. (2007). Business groups: An integrated model to focus future research. *Journal of Management Studies, 44*(8), 1551–1579.
Zaheer, S., & Nachum, L. (2011). Sense of place: From location resources to MNE locational capital. *Global Strategy Journal, 1*(1–2), 96–108.
Zaheer, A., Gulati, R., & Nohria, N. (2000). Strategic networks. *Strategic Management Journal, 21*(3), 203.
Zaheer, S. (1995). Overcoming the liability of foreignness. *Academy of Management Journal, 38*(2), 341–363.
Zaheer, S., Lamin, A., & Subramani, M. (2009). Cluster capabilities or ethnic ties & quest; Location choice by foreign and domestic entrants in the services offshoring industry in India. *Journal of International Business Studies, 40*(6), 944–968.
Zheng, P. (2011). The determinants of disparities in inward FDI flows to the three macro-regions of China. *Post-Communist Economies, 23*(02), 257–270.

3

Empirical Literature on the Specific Motivations of FDI

Abstract Locational factors relate to those indicators that influence the pattern of FDI flows. These indicators also are known as economic and noneconomic determinants or push and pull factors. IB scholars have however noted that different types of FDI are driven by different sets of factors. This chapter provides a review of literature on different locational factors of FDI, considering the heterogeneity of host and home locations. This will identify different locational factors by which FDI-specific motivations are determined.

Keywords Market • Efficiency • Strategic • Locational

Locational Factors of FDI

MNEs are attracted to host locations by different locational factors to meet their different strategic needs (Buckley et al. 2007; Zheng and Tan 2011). Several scholarly researches have been conducted along these lines to examine and identify what locational factors are important for FDI. IB scholars have favoured a positive association between market-related

O. Igbinigie et al., *Strategic Motivations of Inward R&D FDI*,
https://doi.org/10.1007/978-3-030-41015-5_3

factors and FDI into developing countries by advanced countries' MNEs and EM MNEs. For example, Büthe and Milner (2008) examine the effects of GDP growth and per capita GDP on FDI for 122 developing countries from 1970 to 2000. The study estimates reveal a statistically significant positive effect of GDP growth on FDI inflows, while population size and per capita GDP effects were not statistically significant. Okafor (2015) used panel data techniques to investigate the locational determinants of US outward foreign direct investment (FDI) into 23 countries of sub-Saharan Africa (SSA) for 1996–2010. The study found a significant positive causal relationship between GDP per capita, population growth, and US MNEs' FDI into SSA. Bevan and Estrin (2004) examined the determinants of FDI from Western countries mainly from the European Union to Central and Eastern European Countries. The study reported a positive relationship between GDP and FDI inflows into Eastern and Central Europe. Zheng (2013) employed panel dataset at the aggregate country level to examine the variation in the patterns of Indian inward FDI. The study found a significant positive relationship between relative market growth (proxied by GDP growth) and inward FDI from both OECD countries and non-OECD countries.

Similarly, Zheng and Tan (2011) reported a significant positive relationship between Chinese market growth and FDI from member states of the Organization for Economic Co-operation and Development countries. However, De Beule and Van Den Bulcke (2012) reported a significant negative effect of per capita GDP on the number of Greenfield investments by both Indian and Chinese firms. In contrast, Wernick et al. (2009) analysed 64 emerging markets' FDI inflows and reported that GDP per capita has a negative effect on FDI inflows. Based on industry-level data, Rastogi and Sawhney (2014) reveal that market size is positively related to FDI into Indian manufacturing industry particularly FDI from Singapore and the US, while a negative effect was found for UK MNEs' FDI into the Indian manufacturing industry.

In terms of FDI into developed countries either by EM MNEs or other developed countries' MNEs, studies using country-level and firm-level data also found positive effects of market size on FDI. For example, Bagchi-Sen and Wheeler (1989) examined the importance of population size, population growth rate, and per capita retail sales on FDI into the spatial distribution among metropolitan areas in the US. The study found that population size, population growth rate, and per capita retail sales are essential determinants of the spatial distribution of FDI among metropolitan areas in the US. Bilgili et al. (2012) analysed the major determinants of FDI with quarterly dataset of Turkey between 1988 and 2010. The study recorded a positive and statistically significant effect of GDP growth rate on FDI. In the same vein, Castellani et al. (2014) found a positive relationship between population density, per capita GDP, and FDI inflows into the EU service sector. For R&D FDI, Kumar (2001) investigated the determinants of US and Japanese's MNEs' R&D FDI activities and found that large domestic market with potentials such as high per capita income level is a favourable factor of R&D FDI. Von Zedtwitz and Gassmann (2002) showed that R&D activities are located in close proximity to the market and science. They noted that access to the market where customers' perception or changes in consumers' demand can be easily detected helps the firm stay at the forefront of market developments. Athukorala and Kohpaiboon (2010) also found that R&D intensity of US MNE foreign affiliates are determined mainly by domestic market size (proxied by real GDP; geographic distance between the US and the host country; domestic market orientation of MNE affiliates measured by the percentage of domestic sales in total sales turnover of affiliates) coupled with overall R&D capability and the cost of hiring R&D personnel. In another related study, Erdogan and Unver (2015) using a dynamic panel data analysis of 88 countries for both developed and developing countries found a positive and significant relationship between market size (proxy by per capita GPD) and FDI. Erdogan and Unver (2015) further revealed that the ratio of population over the age of 65 has a significant negative effect on FDI.

Another important locational determinant for FDI is human capital. Theoretically, IB scholars argued that MNE is drawn to a particular location due to the availability of highly skilled labour or lower labour cost or high labour productivity level (Noorbakhsh et al. 2001; Habib and Zurawicki 2002; Zheng 2011). These authors suggest that countries with greater levels of labour resources become a better location for FDI. Thus, labour cost would be an attractive factor for foreign direct investments (particularly when labour cost is synonymous to labour productivity).

Otherwise, high labour cost may discourage foreign investments. Awate et al. (2014) and Zhou (2016) noted that MNEs favour locations with a higher proportion of scientists, engineers, or higher education graduates. Bevan and Estrin (2004) found that labour cost has to be negatively related to FDI after investigating FDI from Western European countries to Central and Eastern European countries. Lewin et al. (2009) documented that shortage of highly skilled science and engineering talent partially explains the relocation of product development from the US to other parts of the world, most notably Asian countries. Billington (1999) and Fallon and Cook (2010, 2014) investigated UK regions, including measures for higher and secondary education to account for human capital; their results suggest that higher education and secondary education have a positive influence on foreign investments in UK regions. Wang (2010) examined data for 26 OECD countries over 11 years' period and reported that tertiary education and the proportion of scientific researchers were the most positive determinants of R&D intensity. In contrast, Papanastassiou and Pearce (1992) failed to find support for secondary education in the case of the US.

Providing evidence from developing countries, Noorbakhsh et al. (2001) used two variables as proxies for human capital (secondary school enrolment and wage costs) on FDI inflows to developing countries. The study recorded significant positive results for secondary school enrolment and FDI, while an insignificant result for wage costs. A study by Sun et al. (2002) examined 20 Chinese regions using a dynamic panel data model; the study revealed that wage cost (measured by average wage cost divided by retail price index) is negatively related to FDI into Chinese regions. The study also reported an insignificant result for education (measured by population with primary school education, junior school education, senior secondary school education). Okafor (2015) found that primary education (completion rate) is positively related to US MNEs' FDI in sub-Saharan Africa. Wahid et al. (2009) examined FDI inflow into Africa, and Egger and Winner (2005) examined 73 countries of both developed and developing countries; both found similar results that secondary school enrolment has statistically significant positive effects on FDI inflows.

In contrast, Majeed and Ahmad (2008) after examining 23 developing countries covering 35 years (1970–2004) found a negative relationship between illiteracy and FDI. Hecock and Jepsen (2013) in a study of 58 developing countries found no empirical evidence of the effect of secondary school enrolment on FDI inflows. However, Khan and Veliyath (2011) examined R&D FDI into emerging market and revealed that greater availability of human capital is associated with greater foreign R&D inflows. Using different measures on different countries or regions, some other authors confirmed the positive impact of labour characteristics and FDI. For example, Villaverde and Maza (2015) found a positive relationship between labour market characteristics and FDI into 260 EU NUTS2 regions but reported an insignificant result for labour regulation. Castellani et al. (2014) found that human capital and wage cost are positively related to FDI in the service sector of EU NUTS2 regions. Jaumotte and Pain (2005) using panel data for 20 OECD countries from 1980 to 2001 found that the main determinants of innovativeness were the availability of scientists and engineers, in addition to other factors like publicly funded research, business academia partnerships, and the degree of product market competitiveness.

However, Mody and Srinivasan (1998) noted that during the 1980s, the US and Japanese multinationals were attracted by some similar country characteristics like low wage, inflation, and highly educated workforce. Friedman et al. (1997) also found that skilled labour measured by per capita number of scientists and engineers have a significant impact on the location of foreign branch plants in the US. The study also revealed that wage cost (and per capita number of scientists and engineers) is negative (positive) and significantly related to FDI in high-tech sectors. However, wage costs and engineers per capita become insignificant in the low high-tech sector. Further analyses on source country-level data revealed that per capita number of scientists and engineers are positively related to manufacturing FDI by Japan and EU MNEs, but insignificant results were recorded for other firms. In contrast, evidence from developing countries has documented a negative effect of labour characteristics on FDI. For example, Narula and Wakelin (1998) based on a sample of 22 developing countries investigated the effects of technological capabilities (measured as the number of patents as a ratio of the number of students at the tertiary level) and human capital (measured as a ratio of total student enrolment at the tertiary level to total population). The study found a negative and significant impact of technological capabilities, while a positive but insignificant impact was reported for human capital. Feenstra and Hanson (1997) investigated the impact of human capital (proxied by adult literacy rates) on FDI inflows and found that political stability and property rights are more important determinants than human capital. Kinoshita and Campos (2003) reported a negative relationship between wages (measured by gross nominal wage) and FDI. However, the level of human capital could also be associated with unemployment level or unemployment claimants as an indicator of locational factors in FDI study. High unemployment level or unemployment claimants may impact on labour cost (negatively) and may, in turn, attract foreign investments (Fallon and Cook 2010, 2014). That is, lower labour cost due to high unemployment may reflect lower-skilled labour (where labour cost in itself reflects labour productivity). Erdogan and Unver (2015) used a panel data of 88 countries of both developed and developing countries and found that the unemployment rate and labour force growth rate are positively related to FDI.

Another relevant locational indicator for FDI is agglomeration. According to Sun et al. (2002), agglomeration refers to the co-location and concentration of economic activities that give rise to economies of scale and positive externalities. Theoretically, IB scholars argued that the level of agglomeration in a particular location should be positively related to the FDI (Cantwell and Piscitello 2002; Belderbos et al. 2014). Cantwell and Piscitello (2002) and Chung and Alcácer (2002) argued that firms are attracted to locations as a result of the presence of inter-organisational knowledge due to pool of specialised labour and innovation opportunities to improve their innovative performance. Belderbos et al. (2014) further pointed out that undertaking R&D activity in technology clusters, firms get access to field-specific knowledge and can improve the productivity of their R&D activities. Another perspective to this is that MNE activity in a host location may be related to past activity in that location or localisation of existing R&D activities in that location (self-reinforcing feedback effect) (Jensen et al. 2007; Zheng 2011). Braunerhjelm and Svensson (1996) showed that agglomeration (measured by the share of employees in an industry to all employees in the manufacturing sector) is positively associated with Swedish MNC location of FDI. Wheeler and Mody (1992) also revealed that agglomeration proxied by infrastructure quality (GDP per square kilometre, highway and railway mileage per square kilometre), the degree of industrialisation (domestic investment per worker), and cumulative foreign investment (the ratio of the cumulative FDI relative to the cumulative domestic investment) positively attracts FDI. As revealed in Combes (2000), Van (2002), and Burger et al. (2008), localisation externalities are positively related to services than to other sectors, suggesting that services benefit more from concentration than other economic activities. Adding to that, Antonietti and Cainelli (2008) reported that spatial agglomeration (measured by the probability of finding specialised external providers, face-to-face contacts, and close spatial interaction) positively affects the location of business services in Italy. Marek (2012) documented that localisation externalities, as well as R&D and patenting activity, are among the key determinants for the location of foreign firms in Germany.

As per the noneconomic locational factor, authors have identified the level of technological activities and technological infrastructure to influence FDI. Here, IB scholars argued that host country with high technological capabilities attracts more FDI than countries with low technological capabilities (Dunning 1998; Archibugi and Coco 2004). As suggested in Archibugi and Coco (2004), technological capabilities of a country are composed of a variety of sources of knowledge and of innovation which usually accounts for those activities that are codified as well as tacit. Within the literature, authors have adopted a multidimensional approach for defining technological capabilities embedded in a country; these could be based on the technological activities (e.g. local R&D intensity, patents, or human capital in terms of scientist and engineers as discussed earlier) or quality of technological infrastructures (e.g. roads, internet, and so on) or other measures devised by UN agencies, like the UNDP Human Development Report's Technology Achievement Index (TAI) and UNIDO's Industrial Performance Scoreboard, technology effort index (developed by Lall 2003) and the technology sophistication index and quality of scientific research institute indexes (both from the Global Competitiveness Report). Evidence from both developed and developing countries showed that technological activities and technological infrastructure do influence FDI. For example, Clegg (1987) found that R&D intensity is positively associated with new foreign investment in the UK, Japan, and Germany. Sun et al. (2002) analysed 29 Chinese regions from 1985 to 1995 and revealed that the level of scientific research (measured by R&D expenditures, the number of patents, and the number of universities) has a positive impact on the inflow of FDI to China regions. Athukorala and Kohpaiboon (2010) investigated the determinants of foreign R&D investment by US-based manufacturing MNEs. The study revealed that domestic technological competency measured by technology effort index and R&D personnel per million population is positively associated with R&D FDI, while other variables like the technology sophistication index and quality of scientific research institute indexes were found to be insignificant.

Another variable associated with technological capability is the quality of technological infrastructure. As noted in Kumar (2001), technological resources and infrastructure are key factors that affect the direction of R&D-oriented FDI. Archibugi and Coco (2004) suggested that production knowledge is associated with the availability and diffusion of technological infrastructure. Khan and Veliyath (2011) noted that advances in information and communication technologies (ICTs) are characteristic of the sophistication of the country's technology environment. From a broader perspective, a well-developed infrastructure promotes efficient utilisation of labour force and thus can increase the profits of the firm by reducing the cost of production (Athukorala and Kohpaiboon 2010). Kumar (2001) analysed the determinants of locations of oversea R&D activities of US and Japanese firms. They reported evidence of at least three factors that favoured such location decisions, one among which was the scale of national technological efforts. Polder et al. (2009) reported a complementary effect of ICTs on R&D. However, evidence from developing countries shows contrary results. For example, Khan and Veliyath (2011) investigated R&D FDI in a sample of 26 emerging markets. They hypothesised a negative relationship between technological environment (proxied by share of the population with internet access) and R&D FDI. They found an insignificant positive relationship.

As regards open trade and FDI inflows, there is this consensus among IB scholars that host countries with open trade policies and fewer capital controls are attractive to FDI (Noorbakhsh et al. 2001; Sun et al. 2002; Asiedu and Lien 2004; Büthe and Milner 2008). However, the influence of economic openness on FDI is twofold. On the one hand, a more open economy attracts FDI to welcome foreign capital and foreign investors into the host economy. On the other hand, openness facilitates increase competition among firms attractive to FDI. Noorbakhsh et al. (2001) found a positive relationship between trade openness (measured by credits to the private sector as a percentage of GDP) and FDI inflows. Büthe and Milner (2008) after empirical study of 122 developing countries reported a significant positive relationship between bilateral investment treaties and FDI inflows. Okafor (2015) examined US FDI in sub-Saharan Africa and revealed that trade openness (measured by exports plus imports as a share of GDP) is positively related to FDI by US MNEs. Asiedu and Lien (2004) investigated the effect of capital control policies on FDI and revealed that FDI flow decreased through capital controls. Providing empirical evidence for both developed and developing countries, Yiu et al. (2007) revealed that openness appears to be less important for all economies, while based on individual group analysis, FDI appears to be important for developed economies only. In another related study, Economou et al. (2017) examined 24 OECD countries and 22 developing countries covering a period 1980–2012 using dynamic panel data analysis. The study fails to find significant results for trade openness (proxied by exports plus imports as a percentage of GDP) and FDI inflow.

Another variable associated with economic openness is tariff barriers. Several studies support the view that decreased tariff barriers enhance international trade and intensify global competition (Grossman and Helpman 1991; Khan and Veliyath, 2011). Increased competitiveness thus pushes firms to engage in FDI to retain or expand their market share by offering innovative products of higher quality (Lumenga-Neso et al. 2005; Khan and Veliyath, 2011). Krugman (1984) argued that trade barriers whether in the form of quotas or tariffs could influence firms to increase investments in R&D. An empirical study by Zietz and Fayissa (1992) revealed a positive relationship between increased import competition due to a reduction in trade barriers and increased investments in

R&D in high-tech industries. Khan and Veliyath (2011) noted that increase in tariff rates could also lead to an increased R&D activity in the home country (at least in the short run), especially if the home market size is large and if monopolistic firms are fighting for retention or expansion of market shares. Reitzes (1991) showed that tariffs might lead to increased investments in cost-reducing R&D, while quotas would reduce R&D. Grossman and Helpman (1991) contend that trade liberalisation promotes competition among firms in different countries and thus provides incentives for technological innovation via strengthening R&D activities.

Also, the volatility between the home/host currency exchange rates, inflation, and interest rates has been argued to influence FDI flows. Here, IB scholars proposed a negative relationship between host country exchange rate and FDI inflows (Mody and Srinivasan 1991). These authors argued that low or undervalued exchange rates create more profitable opportunities for inward FDI allowing foreign investors to invest in cheap local assets. Froot and Stein (1989) recorded that appreciation of home currency increases MNCs' wealth position reducing the relative cost of capital and then invests actively in foreign markets. Mody and Srinivasan (1991) distinguishing industry sectors reported that the negative effect of exchange rate fluctuation on FDI is found in some (but not all) industrial sectors. Campa (1993) reported that the devaluation of the Japanese yen (in relation to US dollar) is negatively associated with the number of investments into the US by Japanese MNCs, particularly in industries requiring physical assets. Yol and Teng (2009) find that real appreciation of the Malaysian currency is associated with FDI inflows into Malaysia. Nyarko and Barnor (2011) also reported a positive but insignificant relationship between exchange rate and FDI inflows into Ghana. Put together, it is deduced that there is a consensus that the volatility between the home/host currency exchange rates could influence FDI flows.

Inflation rate and interest rates are used as a proxy for the precariousness of economic atmosphere of the host location. High inflation and interest rates reflect the volatility of the host economic position for investments. Likewise, to currency exchange rate, IB scholars propose a negative relationship between inflation rate and interest rates on FDI

(Li and Liu 2005). The idea here is that if interest rates for borrowing funds are lower in the host country than in the home country, MNCs can raise funds within the host country to support their investments. Buckley et al. (2007) noted that volatile and unpredictable inflation rates in a host country discourage market-seeking FDI by creating uncertainty and making long-term corporate planning problematic, especially in respect of price-setting and profit expectations. Yang et al. (2000) investigating the determinants of FDI in Australia found that high-interest rates are negatively significant with FDI in the 1980s and early 1990s. Li and Liu (2005) found that inflation rates are negatively associated with FDI inflows based on a sample of 84 countries for the periods between 1970 and 1999. Using different sample groups, the study revealed that a negative effect of inflation was only robust in developing countries, while effect of inflation was negative but not significant in developed countries. Asiedu (2002) suggested that the negative relationship between inflation and FDI in a sample of developing countries is because those countries have continually exhibited high inflation rates and extreme budget deficits, which serve as a signal to foreign investors about the unreliability of such economies. However, Asiedu (2002) and Gedik (2013) found no statistically significant relationship in their study.

Another dominant driver of FDI inflows can be attributed to an analysis of the political landscape of the host/home location. This may relate to the level of corruption, regulatory quality, and the level of political stability or instability. Although there is no consensus among researchers about relevant measures of institutional quality, several measures associated with institutional factors of the host countries are identified in the literature. As noted in Erdogan and Unver (2015), corruption variable, as a measure of institutional quality, shows the level of nepotism, excessive patronage, and bribery in the political system. Egger and Winner (2005) after investigating a sample of 73 developed and less-developed countries revealed a positive relationship between corruption and FDI. This indicates that corruption is thus a stimulus for FDI. In contrast, Hecock and Jepsen (2013) came up with negative and statistically significant results. Habib and Zurawicki (2002) reported that the lower the perception of corruption, the higher the FDI inflows after controlling for political stability, transparency index, and absolute difference of corruption perception. Wei (2000) also reported that corruption decreases FDI inflows, indicating that investors are averse to corruption. Brouthers et al. (2008) tried to find the effect of the interaction between corruption and market attractiveness in the different types of FDI. They hypothesised and found that for market-seeking FDI the extra costs corruption creates can be offset by increasing price in markets where customers are less sensitive to price. However, for resource-seeking FDI, the compensatory relationship between corruption and market attractiveness does not hold for resource-seeking FDI because "there is a limit to how cheap resources can be, but no limit to how much corruption can cost" (p. 675). Cazurra (2008) tried to answer why transition economies show high corruption and also high FDI inflows despite the negative impact of corruption on FDI. Cazurra (2008) first examined the effect of corruption on FDI inflows and found that corruption is negatively associated with FDI. Also, using an interaction variable between the host country's level of corruption and host country's transition economy, Cazurra (2008) reported the coefficient on the interaction term is positive and statistically significant, indicating that corruption negatively influences FDI, but its impact is smaller in transition countries than in the other countries. Moreover, arguing that different types of corruption in the host country may have different impacts on FDI, Cazurra (2008) distinguished pervasive corruption (representing the known costs of corruption) and arbitrary corruption (representing the uncertainty associated with corruption) and reported pervasive and arbitrary corruption both have negative impacts on FDI. Using the interaction terms between each type of corruption and a host country's transition economy, Cazurra (2008) found pervasive corruption has a more significant negative impact on FDI in transition countries than in the other countries, while arbitrary corruption has a smaller negative impact.

In addition to corruption, another variable associated with institutional factors is the rule of law. Brunetti et al. (1997) examined the rule of law and corruption by showing that the variables are the highest two factors associated with economic and political uncertainty. They reported both the rule of law and corruption to having a strong negative effect on private investment. Globerman and Shapiro (2003) examining 143 countries of US FDI from 1995 to 1997 noted that the quality of governance infrastructure (representing attitudes of legislation, regulation, and legal system) is a key factor in attracting US FDI. Employing a two-stage estimation procedure, they found that a country that is below the minimum threshold of effective governance is not likely to get US FDI. They conclude that host country investments in governance infrastructure not only attracted capital but also created the conditions under which domestic MNEs emerge and invest abroad. Wernick et al. (2009) investigated the effect of the quality of governance institutions on FDI inflows in 64 emerging economies over 1996 to 2006. The study revealed that institutional quality is a key factor for drawing FDI and concluded that countries that wish to increase the level of FDI should secure intellectual and property rights and ease bureaucracies and crackdown on corruption, lawlessness, and human rights.

Another variable associated with institutional quality is intellectual right protection and political stability. Theoretically, weak intellectual property right protection and high political risk are generally associated with low FDI. Khan and Veliyath (2011) in a study of R&D FDI in 26 countries from 1990 to 2002 found that patent rights index is positively associated with R&D FDI. Kumar (1996) found inconsistent evidence on the role of intellectual property protection effect on R&D activity of US MNEs. Here, their results showed a significant positive effect for the industrialised countries but insignificant effect for the developing countries. On the other hand, Loree and Guisinger (1995) reported a significant positive association between the political stability of the recipient location and US FDI. Nigh (1985) reported that political instability is a strong deterrent factor of FDI only in developing countries, but not in developed countries. However, Sethi et al. (2002) and Asiedu (2002) found no impact of political instability on FDI.

The geographical proximity between the home and host countries could also influence FDI flows (Johanson and Wiedersheim-Paul 1975; Johanson and Vahlne 1977). As MNEs export in less familiar foreign markets, the MNC obtains enough experience and knowledge about the foreign markets and after some time will then set up a direct subsidiary operating in foreign markets. Greater distance causes transportation costs to increase; thus, there is a substitution of FDI for other modes as distance increases. Using distance between the centres of the home and host country in miles, Cazurra (2008) revealed that there is a negative relationship between distance and FDI. Authors have also hypothesised that the effect of distance may be different across types of FDI. For example, Fukao and Wei (2008) revealed that the greater the distance is, the less the vertical FDI to occur. Opposite results were found for horizontal FDI, indicating that greater distance promotes horizontal FDI. The results indicate that greater distance means higher transportation costs and in turn increase in trade costs. As such, it encourages firms to produce goods abroad instead of serving host markets through export. In terms of R&D FDI, the geographical distance may induce MNEs to undertake R&D for product adaptation with closer proximity to its consumer base Athukorala and Kohpaiboon (2010). However, Athukorala and Kohpaiboon (2010) noted that R&D activities of MNE affiliates should depend positively on the extent to which the host country market is served from local production. Such that the impact of domestic market orientation on local R&D effort may depend on the differences in demand conditions between the host country and regional markets and the degree of market segmentation result from tariff and non-tariff barriers couple with if the firm is either market-seeking or technology-seeking (Athukorala and Kohpaiboon 2010).

Also, strong socio-economic connections across national borders have been argued to influence the pattern of FDI. Cultural similarity allows for an MNE to be risk averse in investing in foreign markets (Chung 1991). As noted by Buckley et al. (2007), Chinese in the diaspora have been acknowledged to have contributed to the integration of China into the world economy since 1979. For instance, several scholars argue that ethnic and family Guanxi networks constitute a firm-specific advantage for Chinese MNEs because this helps to reduce the business risk and transaction costs (Erdener and Shapiro 2005) associated with the identification of business opportunities in specific foreign markets (Zhan 1995). However, different measures have been employed by previous studies to analyse cultural distance (e.g. common language used by Cazurra [2008]; country dummy used by Chung [1991]; Hofstede's four dimensions of culture used by Habib and Zurawicki [2002]). However, it is worth noting that empirical findings of cultural distance have been inconsistent. While Cazurra (2008) found a positive and statistically significant effect of common language on FDI, the study by Habib and Zurawicki (2002) reported a negative but not significant effect of cultural distance.

Taken as a whole, the reviewed literature on the locational determinants of FDI and R&D FDI showed that MNEs are attracted to host locations by different locational factors to meet their different strategic needs (Buckley et al. 2007; Zheng and Tan 2011). Scholarly studies have shown that these locational factors could be linked to locational motivations such as market-seeking, efficiency-seeking, strategic asset-seeking, and resource-seeking FDI (Dunning 1998; Von Zedtwitz and Gassmann 2002, Fallon and Cook 2010, 2014).

Conclusion

This chapter provides an extensive review of the empirical literature of determinants of FDI and R&D FDI. From this, it has been observed that the heterogeneity of MNE and their specific capabilities allow the MNE to invest in foreign locations to exploit or augment the competitive advantage. The next chapter will thus develop the study conceptual and analytical framework.

References

Antonietti, R., & Cainelli, G. (2008). Spatial agglomeration, technology and outsourcing of knowledge-intensive business services: Empirical insights from Italy. *International Journal of Services Technology and Management, 10*(2–4), 273–298.

Archibugi, D., & Coco, A. (2004). A new indicator of technological capabilities for developed and developing countries. *World Development, 32*(4), 629–654.

Asiedu, E. (2002). On the determinants of foreign direct investment to developing countries: Is Africa different? *World Development, 30*(1), 107–119.

Asiedu, E., & Lien, D. (2004). Capital controls and foreign direct investment. *World Development, 32*(3), 479–490.

Athukorala, P., & Kohpaiboon, A. (2010). Globalization of R&D by US-based multinational enterprises. *Research Policy, 39*(10), 1335–1347.
Awate, S., Larsen, M. M., & Mudambi, R. (2014). Accessing vs sourcing knowledge: A comparative study of R&D internationalization between emerging and advanced economy firms. *Journal of International Business Studies, 46*(1), 63–86.
Bagchi-Sen, S., & Wheeler, J. O. (1989). A spatial and temporal model of foreign direct investment in the United States. *Economic Geography, 65*(2), 113–129.
Belderbos, R., Van Roy, V., Leten, B., & Thijs, B. (2014). Academic research strengths and multinational firms' foreign R&D location decisions: Evidence from R&D investments in European regions. *Environment and Planning A, 46*(4), 920–942.
Bevan, A. A., & Estrin, S. (2004). The determinants of foreign direct investment into European transition economies. *Journal of Comparative Economics, 32*(4), 775–787.
Bilgili, F., Tülüce, N. S. H., & Doğan, İ. (2012). The determinants of FDI in Turkey: A Markov regime-switching approach. *Economic Modelling, 29*(4), 1161–1169.
Billington, N. (1999). The location of foreign direct investment: An empirical analysis. *Applied Economics, 31*(1), 65–76.
Braunerhjelm, P., & Svensson, R. (1996). Host country characteristics and agglomeration in foreign direct investment. *Applied Economics, 28*(7), 833–840.
Brouthers, L. E., Gao, Y., & McNicol, J. P. (2008). Corruption and market attractiveness influences on different types of FDI. *Strategic Management Journal, 29*(6), 673–680.
Brunetti, A. A. O., Kisunko, G., & Weder, B. S. (1997). *Institutional obstacles to doing business: region-by-region results from a worldwide survey of the private sector*. World Bank Policy Research Working Paper, no. 1759.
Buckley, P. J., Clegg, L. J., Cross, A. R., Liu, X., Voss, H., & Zheng, P. (2007). The determinants of Chinese outward foreign direct investment. *Journal of International Business Studies, 38*(4), 499–518.
Burger, M. J., Van Oort, F. G., & Van der Knaap, B. (2008). *A treatise on the geographical scale of agglomeration externalities and the modifiable areal unit problem*. ERIM Report Series Research in Management, no. ERS-2008-076.
Büthe, T., & Milner, H. V. (2008). The politics of foreign direct investment into developing countries: Increasing FDI through international trade agreements? *American Journal of Political Science, 52*(4), 741–762.

Campa, J. M. (1993). Entry by foreign firms in the United States under exchange rate uncertainty. *The Review of Economics and Statistics, 15*(8), 614–622.

Cantwell, J., & Piscitello, L. (2002). The location of technological activities of MNCs in European regions: The role of spillovers and local competencies. *Journal of International Management, 8*(1), 69–96.

Castellani, D., Meliciani, V., & Mirra, L. (2014). The determinants of inward foreign direct investment in business services across European regions. *Regional Studies, 50*(04), 1–21.

Chung, K. J. (1991). *The distribution patterns of US foreign direct investment: Sensitivity of locational and policy variables by dynamic features of international investments*. Ph.D. Thesis, University of Texas.

Chung, W., & Alcácer, J. (2002). Knowledge seeking and location choice of foreign direct investment in the United States. *Management Science, 48*(12), 1534–1554.

Clegg, J. (1987). *Multinational enterprise and world competition: a comparative study of the USA, Japan, the UK, Sweden and West Germany*. Springer.

Combes, P. (2000). Economic structure and local growth: France, 1984–1993. *Journal of Urban Economics, 47*(3), 329–355.

Cazurra, A. (2008). Better the devil you don't know: Types of corruption and FDI in transition economies. *Journal of International Management, 14*(1), 12–27.

De Beule, F., & Van Den Bulcke, D. (2012). Locational determinants of outward foreign direct investment: An analysis of Chinese and Indian greenfield investments. *Transnational Corporations, 21*(1), 1–34.

Dunning, J. H. (1998). Location and the multinational enterprise: A neglected factor? *Journal of International Business Studies, 1*(3), 45–66.

Economou, F., Hassapis, C., Philippas, N., & Tsionas, M. (2017). Foreign direct investment determinants in OECD and developing countries. *Review of Development Economics, 21*(3), 527–542.

Egger, P., & Winner, H. (2005). Evidence on corruption as an incentive for foreign direct investment. *European Journal of Political Economy, 21*(4), 932–952.

Erdener, C., & Shapiro, D. M. (2005). The internationalization of Chinese family enterprises and Dunning's eclectic MNE paradigm. *Management and Organization Review, 1*(3), 411–436.

Erdogan, M., & Unver, M. (2015). Determinants of foreign direct investments: Dynamic panel data evidence. *International Journal of Economics and Finance, 7*(5), 82.

Fallon, G., & Cook, M. (2010). Exploring the regional distribution of inbound foreign direct investment in the UK in theory and practice: Evidence from a five-region study. *Regional Studies, 44*(3), 337–353.
Fallon, G., & Cook, M. (2014). Explaining manufacturing and non-manufacturing inbound FDI location in five UK regions. *Royal Dutch Geographical Society KNA, 105*(3), 331–348.
Feenstra, R. C., & Hanson, G. H. (1997). Foreign direct investment and relative wages: Evidence from Mexico's maquiladoras. *Journal of International Economics, 42*(3), 371–393.
Friedman, J., Gerlowski, D. A., & Silberman, J. (1997). Foreign direct investment: The factors affecting the location of foreign branch plants in the United States. *Global Finance Journal, 7*(2), 209–222.
Froot, K. A., & Stein, J. C. (1989). Exchange rates and foreign direct investment: an imperfect capital markets approach. *The quarterly journal of economics, 106*(4), 1191–1217.
Fukao, K., & Wei, Y. (2008). *How do the location determinants of vertical FDI and horizontal FDI differ?* Federal Reserve Bank of St Louis, DEAS Working Paper Series from RePEc.
Gedik, M. A. (2013). Determinants of foreign direct investment for OECD countries: Evidence from dynamic panel data analysis. *British Journal of Economics, Finance and Management Sciences, 7*(2), 119–140.
Globerman, S., & Shapiro, D. (2003). Governance infrastructure and US foreign direct investment. *Journal of International Business Studies, 34*(1), 19–39.
Grossman, G., & Helpman, E. (1991). *Innovation and growth in the global economy.* Cambridge: MIT press.
Habib, M., & Zurawicki, L. (2002). Corruption and foreign direct investment. *Journal of International Business Studies, 7*(2), 291–307.
Hecock, R. D., & Jepsen, E. M. (2013). Should countries engage in a race to the bottom? The effect of social spending on FDI. *World Development, 44*, 156–164.
Jaumotte, F., & Pain, N. (2005). *From Ideas to Development: The Determinants of R&D and Patenting.* OECD Economics Department Working Paper, no. 457.
Jensen, J., Rutherford, T, & Tarr, D. (2007). The impact of liberalizing barriers to foreign direct investment in services: the case of Russian accession to the World Trade Organization. *Review of Development Economics, 11*(3), 482–506.
Johanson, J, & Wiedersheim-Paul, F. (1975). The internationalization of the firm: Four Swedish cases, *Journal of Management Studies, 12*(3), 305–322

Johanson, J., & Vahlne, J. (1977). The internationalization process of the firm-a model of knowledge development and increasing foreign market commitments. *Journal of International Business Studies, 2*(7), 23–32.
Khan, A.M., Roy, A.K. and Veliyath, R. (2011) Globalization and International R&D Flows into Emerging Markets: Nomothetic Evidence. *Journal of Emerging Knowledge in Emerging Markets, 3*(9), 118–141.
Kinoshita, Y., & Campos, N. F. (2003). *Why does FDI go where it goes? New evidence from the transition economies*. IMF Working Paper, WP/03/228.
Krugman, P. (1984). Import protection as export promotion: International competition in the presence of oligopoly and economies of scale. In Henryk Kterzskowskl (ed.). *Monopolistic competition and international trade*, 180–193.
Kumar, N. (1996) Intellectual property protection, market orientation and location of overseas R&D activities by multinational enterprises. *World Development 24*(4), 673–688.
Kumar, N. (2001). Determinants of location of overseas R&D activity of multinational enterprises: The case of US and Japanese corporations. *Research Policy, 30*(1), 159–174.
Lall, S. (2003). Indicators of the relative importance of IPRs in developing countries. *Research Policy, 32*(9), 1657–1680.
Lewin, A. Y., Massini, S., & Peeters, C. (2009). Why are companies offshoring innovation? The emerging global race for talent. *Journal of International Business Studies, 40*(6), 901–925.
Li, X., & Liu, X. (2005). Foreign direct investment and economic growth: An increasingly endogenous relationship. *World Development, 33*(3), 393–407.
Loree, D. W., & Guisinger, S. E. (1995). Policy and non-policy determinants of US equity foreign direct investment. *Journal of International Business Studies, 26*(2), 281–299.
Lumenga-Neso, O., Olarreaga, M., & Schiff, M. (2005). On indirect trade-related R&D spillovers. *European Economic Review, 49*(7), 1785–1798.
Majeed, M. T., & Ahmad, E. (2008). Human capital development and FDI in developing countries. *Journal of Economic Cooperation, 29*(3), 79–104.
Marek, P. (2012). Agglomeration and FDI in east German knowledge-intensive business services. *Economia politica, 29*(3), 343–360.
Mody, A., & Srinivasan, T. (1991). Trends and determinants of foreign direct investment: analysis of US investment abroad. Washington DC: The World Bank, Industrial Development Division.
Mody, A., & Srinivasan, K. (1998). Japanese and US firms as foreign investors: Do they march to the same tune? *Canadian Journal of Economics, 31*(4), 778–799.

Narula, R., & Wakelin, K. (1998). Technological competitiveness, trade and foreign direct investment. *Structural change and economic dynamics, 9*(3), 373–387.

Nigh, D. (1985). The effect of political events on United States direct foreign investment: A pooled time-series cross-sectional analysis. *Journal of International Business Studies, 16*(00002), 1–17.

Noorbakhsh, F., Paloni, A., & Youssef, A. (2001). Human capital and FDI inflows to developing countries: New empirical evidence. *World Development, 29*(9), 1593–1610.

Nyarko, P. A., & Barnor, C. (2011). Effects of exchange rate regimes on FDI inflows in Ghana. *International Journal of Economics and Finance, 3*(3), 277–281.

Okafor, G. (2015). Locational determinants of us outward FDI into sub-saharan Africa. *The Journal of Developing Areas, 49*(1), 187–205.

Papanastassiou, M., & Pearce, R. D. (1992). Motivation and market strategies of US foreign direct investments: An analysis of host-country determinants. *Global Competition and Technology, 165*, 51–77.

Polder, M., van Leeuwen, G., Mohnen, P., & Raymond, W. (2009). Productivity effects of innovation modes. *Statistics Netherlands discussion paper*, 9033.

Rastogi, R., & Sawhney, A. (2014). *What Attracts FDI in Indian Manufacturing Industries?* Berlin Working Papers on Money, Finance, Trade and Development, No. 2/2014.

Reitzes, J. D. (1991). The impact of quotas and tariffs on strategic R&D behavior. *International Economic Review, 32*(4), 985–1007.

Sethi, D., Guisinger, S., Ford, D. L., & Phelan, S. E. (2002). Seeking greener pastures: A theoretical and empirical investigation into the changing trend of foreign direct investment flows in response to institutional and strategic factors. *International Business Review, 11*(6), 685–705.

Sun, Q., Tong, W., & Yu, Q. (2002). Determinants of foreign direct investment across China. *Journal of International Money and Finance, 21*(1), 79–113.

Van, D. M. (2002). *The determinants of export performance in developing countries: The case of Indonesian manufacturing.* Eindhoven Centre for Innovation Studies Working Paper, 2(01).

Villaverde, J., & Maza, A. (2015). The determinants of inward foreign direct investment: Evidence from the European regions. *International Business Review, 24*(2), 209–223.

Von Zedtwitz, M., & Gassmann, O. (2002). Market versus technology drive in R&D internationalization: four different patterns of managing research and development. *Research policy, 31*(4), 569–588.

Wahid, A.N., Sawkut, R. and Seetanah, B. (2009) Determinants of Foreign Direct Investments (FDI): Lessons from the African Economies. *The Journal of Applied Business and Economics, 9*(1), 70.

Wang, E. C. (2010). Determinants of R&D investment: The extreme-bounds-analysis approach applied to 26 OECD countries. *Research Policy, 39*(1), 103–116.

Wernick, D. A., Haar, J., & Singh, S. (2009). Do governing institutions affect foreign direct investment inflows? *International Journal of Economic and Business Research, 1*(3), 317–332.

Wei, S. (2000). How taxing is corruption on international investors? *Review of economics and statistics, 82*(1), 1–11.

Wheeler, D., & Mody, A. (1992). International investment location decisions: The case of US firms. *Journal of International Economics, 33*(1), 57–76.

Yang, J. Y. Y., Groenewold, N., & Tcha, M. (2000). The determinants of foreign direct investment in Australia. *Economic Record 76*(232), 45–54.

Yiu, D. W., Lu, Y., Bruton, G. D., & Hoskisson, R. E. (2007). Business groups: An integrated model to focus future research. *Journal of Management Studies, 44*(8), 1551–1579.

Yol, M. A., & Teng, N. T. (2009). Estimating the domestic determinants of foreign direct investment flows in Malaysia: Evidence from Cointegration and error-correction model. *Jurnal Pengurusan, 28*(1), 3–22.

Zhan, J. X. (1995). Transnationalization and outward investment: the case of Chinese firms. *Transnational Corporations, 4*, 67–100.

Zheng, P. (2011). The determinants of disparities in inward FDI flows to the three macro-regions of China. *Post-Communist Economies, 23*(2), 257–270.

Zheng, P. (2013). The variation in Indian inward FDI patterns. *Management International Review, 53*(6), 819–839.

Zheng, P., & Tan, H. (2011). Home economy heterogeneity in the determinants of China's inward foreign direct investment. *Transnational Corporations, 20*(2), 1–29.

Zhou, Y. (2016). Drivers of globalization of R&D investment by US multinational enterprises: Evidence from industry-level data. *International Journal of Economics and Finance, 8*(2), 51–69.

Zietz, J., & Fayissa, B. (1992). R & D expenditures and import competition: Some evidence for the US. *Review of World Economics, 128*(1), 52–66.

4

Conceptual Framework: A Model of R&D FDI Motivations in the UK

Abstract A commonly held view in IB research is that MNE plays a pivotal role in the generation of technology and its transmission across locations. MNE capabilities are often self-created and are uniquely attuned to the firm in its deployment. Within this context, R&D is vital in the creation, adaptation, or adoption of knowledge across different foreign locations. This chapter provides a conceptual framework of the study and some set of hypotheses derived to address the research objective and question. The study tests the theoretical argument that, on the one hand, MNE with home-based capabilities will combine both asset-exploiting and asset-augmenting strategies (OECD countries), whilst, on the other hand, MNE with no home-based capabilities will follow an asset-augmenting strategy only (non-OECD countries).

Keywords Exploitation • Augmentation • Market • Efficiency • Strategic • Assets

O. Igbinigie et al., *Strategic Motivations of Inward R&D FDI*,
https://doi.org/10.1007/978-3-030-41015-5_4

Conceptual Framework and Hypotheses Development

Asakawa and Westney (2013) revealed that Japanese foreign R&D in the pharmaceutical and electronics industries followed a mixed evolutionary path. The study revealed that Japanese MNEs in the pharmaceutical industry invest in R&D abroad before sales and production; on the contrary, electronics MNEs followed the more traditional linear pattern, that is, setting up sales offices, production, and finally R&D. Cantwell et al. (2010) argue that a driving force in this evolutionary process is how MNEs adjust their strategies and structures to counter uncertainty and complexity in the development of their activities and their environment. Cantwell et al. (2010) drawing from Nelson (2002), Nelson and Winter (2009), and North (2005) proposed that firms engage in institutional innovation (in the structure of the MNEs) to counter external uncertainty both at the corporate level and at the subsidiary level. Cantwell and Mudambi (2005) argued that changes in institution create incentives for firms' innovation.

Frost and Zhou (2000) revealed that multinational firms make sequential FDI location decisions by adaptation of existing facilities and operations in response to changes in host country conditions. In other words, the composition of the activity profile of MNEs may co-evolve significantly over time in response to local stimuli. The notion of sequential adaptation is especially relevant in the context of foreign investment in R&D precisely because of the important role played by locational factors in processes of technological innovation. An empirical study by Frost and Zhou (2000) analysis of US R&D facilities of Japanese electronics multinationals revealed that foreign firms are particularly attracted to locations known for producing top-quality scientific research such as Princeton, New Jersey, Cambridge, and Massachusetts.

However, given that competition has become technologically intensive and MNEs' increasing need to have multiple technological competences, R&D FDI-specific motivations in a host location will reflect the subsidiary strategies in that location. The study's theoretical and conceptual framework is supported by theories on the strategic and specific motivations of FDI (Cantwell and Piscitello 2002; Von Zedtwitz and Gassmann 2002; Cantwell and Mudambi 2000, 2005; Dunning 1998, 2002; Zheng

2011; Awate et al. 2015). This study extends this literature strand by employing country-level variables as proxy for each strategic and specific motivation and test complementary set of hypotheses to provide a structural approach to model MNE's R&D behaviour between and within heterogeneous home countries in a single host country.

While the extant literature discussed above is rich in the strategic choice for FDI in R&D, it is weak at offering a detailed structure on the relative importance of specific motivations that define the MNEs' FDI in R&D. In response to this gap, this study aims to determine whether the twin strategies of R&D FDI are subject to different specific motivations. This current study adopts an innovative approach to model the behaviour of MNEs' FDI in R&D at the macro level by aligning strategic motives with specific motivations. Drawing from Dunning (1998, 2002), the specific motives of FDI include resource-seeking, market-seeking, efficient-seeking, and strategic asset-seeking MNEs. These specific motives of FDI can, in turn, be linked to location factors of FDI at the country or industry level (Fallon and Cook 2010, 2014).

As exhibited in Fig. 4.1, the conceptual framework explaining the strategic motivations (home-based asset exploitation and home-based asset augmentation) and specific motivations is reflected in the formulated

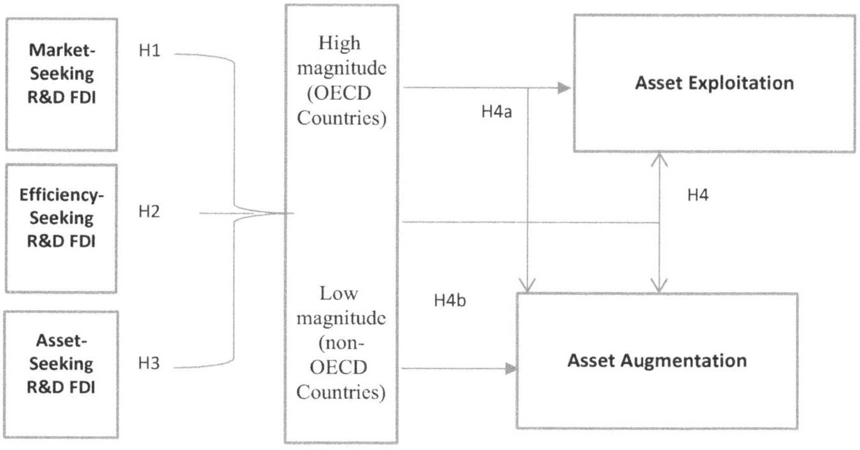

Fig. 4.1 Conceptual framework

Hypotheses H1, H2, H3, H4, H4a, and H4b. Hypotheses H1, H2, and H3 relate to the specific country-level motivations following the theoretical argument in support of location-specific motivations. The study then attempts to integrate particular idiosyncrasies at the country level to MNEs' technological configuration (home-based asset exploitation and home-based asset augmentation) in formulated H4, H4a, and H4b.

In terms of studies in support of location-specific motivations, for example, the importance of market structure and market conditions on inbound FDI is well established within the IB FDI literature (Hill and Munday 1992; Fallon and Cook 2010; Erdogan and Unver 2015). However, little is known empirically on the effects of market structure or market conditions on inbound R&D FDI. As shown in Dunning and Narula (1995) and Falk (2014), market-seeking MNEs can be driven for adaptive R&D FDI in foreign locations when the investing MNE has home-based capabilities. Falk (2014) concludes that when adaptive R&D is the main motive for R&D FDI, the major determinant of firms' location choice is the level of actual or potential demand in the local market. Kumar (2001) document that the determinants of US and Japanese's MNEs R&D activities. Kumar (2001) and Falk (2014) in their studies find that large domestic market with high per capita income level and market size is a favourable factor for R&D FDI for both the US and Japanese MNEs. Athukorala and Kohpaiboon (2010) also find that the R&D intensity of US MNEs' foreign affiliates is determined by domestic market size. This available empirical evidence indicates that locations with high income or high-income growth attract MNEs with pre-existing capabilities for adaptive R&D FDI. However, other studies have shown that firms without pre-existing capabilities may also find it easier to cover the cost of R&D in a location with higher market potentials (Lall 1979; Mansfield et al. 1979; Belderbos et al. 2014). Overall, given the sophistication of UK research base (Cantwell and Mudambi 2000, 2005) and her high market potentials among world-leading nations, the UK may be attractive to market-seeking R&D FDI for asset-exploitation and asset-augmentation R&D activities. MNEs' R&D subsidiaries are located in foreign countries with high market potential either for adaptive R&D (asset exploitation) or to cover the cost of R&D to develop new knowledge (asset augmentation). The UK is attractive to market-seeking R&D FDI either for adaptive or market gains.

H1 *R&D FDI in the UK is determined by market-seeking motivations.*

Dunning and Narula (1995) consider efficiency-seeking R&D as rationalised R&D that is established to capture economies of scale and scope. There are two elements or side to efficiency-seeking R&D FDI; this relates to the quality or the supply of skilled human capital, to gain operational flexibility or cost-related efficiency (Kumar 2001; Athukorala and Kohpaiboon 2010). There is a shared view among IB scholars that high labour cost does discourage foreign investments (Athukorala and Kohpaiboon 2010; Zheng 2011) and high labour skill availability encourages FDI (Awate et al. 2014; Zhou, 2016). For example, lower wages for scientists and engineers located abroad rather than the home country might thus influence MNEs' location decisions. In FDI in R&D literature, there is weak evidence that differences in the cost of R&D personnel are a major driver for the internationalisation of R&D.

Nonetheless, wage differences gain importance when firms consider locating innovative activities in emerging and developing economies (Thursby and Thursby 2006). In the case of advanced economies, R&D FDI activities may largely depend on how well the location meets the human capital requirements of foreign firms. The more relevant skill of labour available locally, the more attractive such location to inward R&D (Billington 1999; Fallon and Cook 2010). Awate et al. (2014) and Zhou (2016) found that MNEs favour locations with a higher proportion of scientists, engineers, or higher education graduates. Kuemmerle (1999) documents that managers favour the availability of outstanding individual researchers, hoping to tap into a high-quality supply of graduate students when setting up R&D units. Adding to that, Bardhan (2006) and Stephan et al. (2008) suggested that MNEs' R&D internationalisation is based to search for not only human capital but also the need for greater firm efficiency and flexibility. Kinkel and Maloca (2008) find that capacity bottlenecks are the most frequent reason why German firms move R&D to foreign locations. Taken as a whole, it, therefore, becomes interesting to empirically ascertain to what extent efficiency-seeking R&D FDI is attracted into the UK.

In R&D FDI research, efficiency-seeking is also referred to as rationalised R&D motivation. However, there are no clear definitions of rationalised R&D motivation and its distinctions under asset-exploitation strategy or asset-augmentation strategy. In this study, efficiency-seeking is considered to depend on how well the host location meets the human capital requirements of foreign firms' R&D FDI activities.

H2 *R&D FDI in the UK is determined by efficiency-seeking motivations.*

Knowledge-intensive activities like R&D do stimulate the ability to identify, assimilate, and exploit innovations. The volume and sophistication of UK's domestic R&D base serve as a conduit for MNEs to source for local knowledge to improve their existing assets or to acquire new knowledge, known in the literature as strategic assets. Strategic assets relate to specific scientific and technological expertise present in a host location. The idea here is that MNEs internationalise their foreign R&D mainly to gain access to crucial inputs such as new knowledge and technology that are location specific and are not easily available in their principal or home markets (Von Zedtwitz and Gassmann 2002; Cantwell and Mudambi 2005). Locations with various centres of knowledge can attract MNEs to stimulate innovation, to boost the international competitiveness of the MNEs (Jaffe et al. 1993; Von Zedtwitz and Gassmann 2002; Belderbos et al. 2014). New knowledge sourced from foreign location helps develop technologies and products that serve not only in the host market but also the home and the global markets. The search for strategic assets amplifies the need to locate R&D FDI in well-chosen countries or regions that are more innovative and technologically advanced (Kuemmerle 1999; Dunning 1998). Access to R&D resources and localised knowledge appears to be the dominant motivation for R&D investment in the US and Europe than in less-developed countries. For example, Odagiri and Yasuda (1996) found that Japanese R&D investments were motivated by technology-sourcing motives in the US and Europe and adaptive R&D motives in Asia. Kuemmerle (1999) documented that the strength of the location in science would influence the extent foreign affiliates to exploit existing firm-specific advantages or to build up new firm-specific advantages. Iwasa and Odagiri (2004) found that Japanese foreign affiliates performing R&D in the US have a positive impact on parent firms' patent applications in Japan. Chung and Yeaple (2008) found that locations with greater technical similarity to the US are more attractive to US MNEs. Di Minin et al. (2012) based on a study of five Chinese affiliates in Europe revealed that R&D internationalisation of China MNCs was driven predominantly by learning motives rather than technological innovativeness.

H3 *R&D FDI in the UK is determined by strategic asset-seeking motivations.*

Given the conceptual distinction between home-based asset exploitation strategies and home-based asset augmentation strategies, MNEs' R&D would be expected to have differing specific motives. However, some authors argue that at the subsidiary level MNEs might carry out both strategies in the same foreign geographical location (Kuemmerle 1999; Cantwell 2017). These authors suggest that some MNEs have dynamic capabilities which could reconfigure their competences to home-based asset exploitation and home-based asset augmentation within the same geographical locations. On the other hand, some other authors reveal that the quality of the host location could influence such dual strategies (Criscuolo et al. 2005; Chung and Yeaple 2008; Awate et al. 2014). This, therefore, suggests that MNEs might undertake both asset-exploiting and asset-augmenting activities simultaneously. The processes used to manufacture new products or improve existing products often utilise several technologies and multiple competencies (Criscuolo et al. 2005). Because products are multi-technology based, firms may engage in both asset-augmenting and asset-exploiting activities. Kuemmerle (1999) observes that MNEs that engage in both strategies in the same location will prima facie exchange information between both types of R&D activities. It is therefore pertinent to note that only firms with dynamic capabilities typically MNEs from the advanced country could employ both strategies in the same foreign geographical location. For example, Awate et al. (2014) using a case study of emerging and advanced MNEs revealed that emerging MNE internationalisation is rooted in the firms' overall catch-up strategy to get on par with industry leaders. This, therefore, suggests that MNEs from advanced industrial and highly technological countries (e.g. OECD countries) will then undertake both asset-exploiting and asset-augmenting activities, while

MNEs from less industrial and technological countries will then undertake asset-augmenting R&D activities. It can be deduced that advanced industrial countries like the UK are best placed to offer strategic locational advantages to the investing firms with dynamic capabilities. As a result, MNEs from OECD countries generally have a higher level of R&D FDI over less-developed countries.

It is established that asset-exploiting foreign affiliate engaged in R&D activity will draw from their parent's technological resources as well as their home location's innovation system (Cantwell and Mudambi 2005; Awate et al. 2014). Given that MNEs' parents are often highly embedded in their home location, these linkages determine the firm-specific advantages which can be leveraged in a foreign location (Cantwell and Mudambi 2005; Awate et al. 2014). When a firm engages in asset-exploiting R&D activities in a foreign location, the foreign affiliate tends to adapt and modify their existing technological assets in response to demand conditions. Asset-augmenting R&D activity tends to absorb and acquire new technologies from the localised knowledge within the host location. Asset-seeking for augmenting purpose tends to be after tacit knowledge associated with the host location. Others like Cantwell and Mudambi (2005) and Awate et al. (2014) suggested that asset-exploiting foreign R&D subsidiaries have a higher level of R&D FDI. For this study, it is expected that the empirical results for OECD countries' specific motivation will have a higher magnitude compared to non-OECD countries (as depicted in Fig. 4.1).

H4 *The specific and strategic motivations of R&D FDI in the UK are different between OECD and non-OECD home countries.*

H4a *OECD R&D FDI in the UK is determined by both asset-exploitation and asset-augmentation strategic motivations.*

H4b *Non-OCEDR&D FDI in the UK is determined by asset-augmentation strategic motivations.*

Conclusion

This chapter provides a conceptual framework of the study and some set of hypotheses derived to address the research objective and question. This study examines the strategic and specific motivations of R&D FDI. Here, the study investigates the interactions of specific motivations (i.e. market-seeking, efficiency-seeking, and strategic asset-seeking) to explain strategic motivations (home-based asset-exploitation and home-based asset-augmentation strategies) in R&D FDI. The study tests the theoretical argument that, on the one hand, MNE with home-based capabilities will combine both asset-exploiting and asset-augmenting strategies (OECD countries), while, on the other hand, MNE with no home-based capabilities will follow asset-augmenting strategies (non-OECD countries).

References

Asakawa, K., & Westney, D. E. (2013). Evolutionary perspectives on the internationalisation of R&D in Japanese multinational corporations. *Asian Business & Management, 12*(1), 115–141.

Athukorala, P., & Kohpaiboon, A. (2010). Globalization of R&D by US-based multinational enterprises. *Research Policy, 39*(10), 1335–1347.

Awate, S., Larsen, M. M., & Mudambi, R. (2014). Accessing vs sourcing knowledge: A comparative study of R&D internationalization between emerging and advanced economy firms. *Journal of International Business Studies, 46*(1), 63–86.

Awate, S., Larsen, M. M., & Mudambi, R. (2015). Accessing vs sourcing knowledge: A comparative study of R&D internationalization between emerging and advanced economy firms. *Journal of International Business Studies, 46*(1), 63–86.

Bardhan, A. D. (2006). Managing globalization of R&D: Organizing for offshoring innovation. *Human Systems Management, 25*(2), 103–114.

Belderbos, R., Van Roy, V., Leten, B., & Thijs, B. (2014). Academic research strengths and multinational firms' foreign R&D location decisions: Evidence from R&D investments in European regions. *Environment and Planning A, 46*(4), 920–942.

Billington, N. (1999). The location of foreign direct investment: An empirical analysis. *Applied Economics, 31*(1), 65–76.

Cantwell, J. (2017). FDI location choice: the role of locational ambidexterity. *Multinational Business Review, 25*(1), 28–51.

Cantwell, J., & Mudambi, R. (2000). The location of MNE R&D Activity: The role of investment incentives. *MIR: Management International Review, 40*(1), 127–148.

Cantwell, J., & Mudambi, R. (2005). MNE competence-creating subsidiary mandates. *Strategic Management Journal, 26*(12), 1109–1128.

Cantwell, J., & Piscitello, L. (2002). The location of technological activities of MNCs in European regions: The role of spillovers and local competencies. *Journal of International Management, 8*(1), 69–96.

Cantwell, J., Dunning, J. H., & Lundan, S. M. (2010). An evolutionary approach to understanding international business activity: The co-evolution of MNEs and the institutional environment. *Journal of International Business Studies, 41*(4), 567–586.

Chung, W., & Yeaple, S. (2008). International knowledge sourcing: Evidence from US firms expanding abroad. *Strategic Management Journal, 29*(11), 1207–1224.

Criscuolo, P., Narula, R., & Verspagen, B. (2005). Role of home and host country innovation systems in R&D internationalisation: A patent citation analysis. *Economics of Innovation and New Technology, 14*(5), 417–433.

Di Minin, A., Zhang, J., & Gammeltoft, P. (2012). Chinese foreign direct investment in R&D in Europe: A new model of R&D internationalization? *European Management Journal, 30*(3), 189–203.

Dunning, J. H. (1998). Location and the multinational enterprise: A neglected factor? *Journal of International Business Studies, 1*(3), 45–66.

Dunning, J. H. (2002). *Global capitalism, FDI and competitiveness*. Cheltenham: Edward Elgar Publishing.

Dunning, J. H., & Narula, R. (1995). The R&D activities of foreign firms in the United States. *International Studies of Management & Organization, 25*(1–2), 39–74.

Erdogan, M., & Unver, M. (2015). Determinants of foreign direct investments: Dynamic panel data evidence. *International Journal of Economics and Finance, 7*(5), 82.

Falk, M. (2014). *Determinants of Greenfield foreign direct investment in R&D and related activities*. FIW Research Reports Series no. IV-002.

Fallon, G., & Cook, M. (2010). Exploring the regional distribution of inbound foreign direct investment in the UK in theory and practice: Evidence from a five-region study. *Regional Studies, 44*(3), 337–353.

Fallon, G., & Cook, M. (2014). Explaining manufacturing and non-manufacturing inbound FDI location in five UK regions. *Royal Dutch Geographical Society KNA, 105*(3), 331–348.

Frost, T., & Zhou, C. (2000). The geography of foreign R&D within a host country: An evolutionary perspective on location-technology selection by multinationals. *International Studies of Management & Organization, 30*(2), 10–43.

Hill, S., & Munday, M. (1992). The UK regional distribution of foreign direct investment: Analysis and determinants. *Regional Studies, 26*(6), 535–544.

Iwasa, T., & Odagiri, H. (2004). Overseas R&D, knowledge sourcing, and patenting: An empirical study of Japanese R&D investment in the US. *Research Policy, 33*(5), 807–828.

Jaffe, A. B., Trajtenberg, M., & Henderson, R. (1993). Geographic Localization of Knowledge Spillovers as Evidenced by Patent Citations. *The Quarterly Journal of Economics, 108*(3), 577–598.

Kinkel, S., & Maloca, S. (2008). *R & D relocation overseas sales of German development expertise? Extent and driver of R & D relocation in manufacturing.* ISI working paper No. 45.

Kuemmerle, W. (1999). Foreign direct investment in industrial research in the pharmaceutical and electronics industries-results from a survey of multinational firms. *Research Policy, 28*(2), 179–193.

Kumar, N. (2001). Determinants of location of overseas R&D activity of multinational enterprises: The case of US and Japanese corporations. *Research Policy, 30*(1), 159–174.

Lall, S. (1979) The international allocation of research activity by US multinationals. *Oxford Bulletin of Economics and Statistics, 41*(4), 313–331.

Mansfield, E., Teece, D., & Romeo, A. (1979). Overseas research and development by US-based firms. *Economica, 46*(182), 187–196.

Nelson, R. R. (2002). Bringing institutions into evolutionary growth theory. *Journal of Evolutionary Economics, 12*(1–2), 17–28.

Nelson, R. R., & Winter, S. G. (2009). *An evolutionary theory of economic change.* Cambridge: Harvard University Press.

North, D. C. (2005). *Understanding the process of economic change.* Princeton and Oxford: Princeton University Press.

Odagiri, H., & Yasuda, H. (1996). The determinants of overseas R&D by Japanese firms: An empirical study at the industry and company levels. *Research Policy, 25*(7), 1059–1079.
Stephan, M., Silvia, M., & Arie Y, L. (2008). A dynamic perspective on next-generation offshoring: The global sourcing of science and engineering talent. *The Academy of Management Perspectives, 22*(3), 35–54.
Thursby, J. G., & Thursby, M. C. (2006). *Here or there? A survey of factors in multinational R&D location: Report to the government/university/industry research roundtable*. Washington, DC: National Academies Press.
Von Zedtwitz, M., & Gassmann, O. (2002). Market versus technology drive in R&D internationalization: Four different patterns of managing research and development. *Research Policy, 31*(4), 569–588.
Zheng, P. (2011). The determinants of disparities in inward FDI flows to the three macro-regions of China. *Post-Communist Economies, 23*(02), 257–270.
Zhou, Y. (2016). Drivers of Globalization of R&D Investment by US Multinational Enterprises: Evidence from Industry-Level Data. *International Journal of Economics and Finance, 8*(2), 51–69.

5

Dynamic Panel Data Analysis Techniques

Abstract The purpose of academic research is to discover the truth regarding research enquiry. Scholarly research involves a systematic search, following the art of scientific investigation to gain new knowledge or facts. There are several designs through which the research objective makes contributions to knowledge; research could be exploratory, descriptive, diagnostic, or experimental. However, the choice of research design depends on the theoretical and philosophical tenets suited for the research context, problem, and question. IB is a multicultural, multidimensional, and dynamic field of study that lends itself to a broad range of research designs, methodologies, and methods. This chapter provides the necessary literature backing within the context of IB research on the chosen research design and methods employed in this study.

Keywords Quantitative • Dynamic • Data • Panel • Methods • Research

O. Igbinigie et al., *Strategic Motivations of Inward R&D FDI*,
https://doi.org/10.1007/978-3-030-41015-5_5

The Research Design

The choice of research design depends on the research context, question(s), and prior studies within the research discipline. This study draws its research theoretical and philosophical assumptions from the positivist, quantitative, and deductive research approach. Quantitative and positivistic empirical methods are well established in IB research within the area of macroeconomic determinants and impacts of FDI (Hill and Munday 1992; Fallon and Cook 2010; Erdogan and Unver 2015; Awate et al. 2014; Zhou 2016). Leading journals in IB favours quantitative papers compared to qualitative papers (Welch and Welch 2004; Birkinshaw 2004; Hurmerinta-Peltomäki and Nummela 2006).

Nevertheless, these authors reiterated that IB qualitative research is equally established in exploring the complex plurality of institutional, cultural, and organisational factors (usually at the micro level). However, combining qualitative and quantitative methods in IB research has mainly been criticised for the lack of consistency in the implementation of a triangulation approach between studies (Oppermann 2000; Teddlie and Tashakkori 2003). This perspective supports the choice of quantitative methods as the only approach for this research. Also, the impact of any research work depends on the appropriateness and rigour of the methods used (Scandura and Williams 2000). According to Cheng et al. (2009), advancing IB research goes beyond reformulating novel dependent or independent variables; it is about applying the appropriate theories, concepts, data, and methods to address the research phenomenon. Deductive research approach begins by identifying and reviewing the relevant theory to be tested, developing a set of hypotheses from the theory, and collecting quantitative data for empirical analysis to either accept or reject the hypotheses (Tuli 2010; Soiferman 2010).

Deductive research employs quantitative data to test for causal relationships to either accept or reject a hypothesis (Tuli 2010; Soiferman 2010; Popkewitz 2012; Creswell and Creswell 2017). For this research, hypotheses are developed from an extensive review of literature relating to relevant theories on the strategic and specific motivations of R&D FDI. Validating these theories through deductive process requires quantitative methods of data collection and analytical techniques in line with the positivist and objectivist research paradigm (Tuli 2010; Soiferman 2010; Popkewitz 2012; Creswell and Creswell 2017). The below section outlines the detailed research methods for data collection and analytical techniques used.

Table 5.1 List of home countries

Pooled	OECD	Non-OECD	Dropped
Austria	Austria	Bahrain	Bahamas
Australia	Australia	China	Barbados
Bahrain	Belgium	China	Bermuda
Belgium	Canada	Hong Kong	Cyprus
China	Denmark	India	Luxembourg
Canada	Finland	Kuwait	Malta
China	France	Malaysia	Mauritius
Denmark	Germany	Saudi Arabia	Panama
Finland	Hungary	Singapore	
France	Iceland	South Africa	
Germany	Ireland	UAE	
Hong Kong	Israel		
Hungary	Italy		
Iceland	Japan		
India	South Korea		
Ireland	Mexico		
Israel	Netherlands		
Italy	New Zealand		
Japan	Norway		
South Korea	Poland		
Kuwait	Spain		
Malaysia	Sweden		
Mexico	Switzerland		
Netherlands	Turkey		
New Zealand	US		
Norway			
Poland			
Saudi Arabia			
Singapore			
South Africa			
Spain			
Sweden			
Switzerland			
Turkey			
UAE			
US			

Sample and Data Collection

This research investigates R&D FDI's motivations in the UK. As shown in Table 5.1, the study data series represent 36 home countries for a period of 8 years (2009–2016). The study datasets were organised into three groups. The first group is the UK pool of all the 36 home countries; the second group is OECD countries comprising 25 countries; and the last group is non-OECD countries comprising 11 countries. Initially, the data series covers 44 home countries that performed R&D in the UK. However, eight home countries identified as tax havens were removed to make the balance of 36 countries. This was done to avoid bias results and to maintain a good number of observations sufficient to produce robust estimates.

This research employs quantitative secondary data collected from multiple data sources used as proxies. Example of data collection sources for both predictive and control variables include statistical data released by the office of national statistics—which provide official data used by the government for economic planning and forecast, statistical data from World Bank's World Development Indicators, and so on. The dependent variable dataset was obtained from the FAME database. In FAME, MNEs are identified if it is ultimately owned by a majority shareholder that is of the same nationality as the MNEs' home country. In order to ensure that the ownership of the MNE is valid throughout the observed period (i.e. 2009–2016), the home country of the MNEs was cross-checked with past releases of the MNEs to ensure that no ownership change in terms of nationality has taken place. Also, following OECD definition, MNEs are defined if it holds at least 10% ownership of the foreign subsidiary. After identifying the firms as MNEs, figures for their expenditure on R&D performed in the UK were aggregated at the country level to derive the study-dependent variable. This database and approach have been used by Jones and Temouri (2016) in their study of determinants of FDI in locations considered as a tax haven.

Quantitative secondary data are not usually confronted with the problems associated with collecting primary data, for example, data collected using questionnaires, surveys, and interviews. However, the quality of secondary data for academic research depends on the reliability of the data (i.e. the credibility of the data sources), suitability of the data (i.e. appropriate for the research enquiry), and lastly, adequacy of the data (i.e. the data is available sufficiently for the research period examined) (Quinlan et al. 2019). For this research, all the relevant data were collected from reliable sources used by prior empirical studies in IB research (as explained above). The proxies used for study models are discussed to justify their suitability for the research. Regarding data adequacy, all the relevant were obtained for the period of study with no gaps, and any proxies with insufficient data were dropped.

Data Analytical Techniques

This research estimates the study parameters using panel data analysis. Panel data or longitudinal data is a dataset which allows for exploration of time series and cross-sectional data. Panel data is also viewed as the pooling of observations across sections (denoted as subscript *i*) and over time (denoted as subscript *t*) (Baltagi 2008). The choice of panel data is associated with the accuracy in estimating parameters. From example, panel dataset provides reliable estimates with observation with fewer time series and cross-sectional dimensions compared to pure time series and cross-sectional dataset (Hsiao 2014). Panel data analysis is also robust in controlling the effects of omitted variables in the model; this is associated with the informative power of panel data on both cross-sectional and time series natures. Panel data analysis reduce the likelihood of collinearity among explanatory variables, increase the degree of freedom and sample validity, and improve efficiency with smaller standard errors (Baltagi 2008).

Although the advantages associated with panel data are well established in the literature (Hsiao 2014; Baltagi 2008), the complex structure of panel data also poses some potential experimental problems (Hsiao 2014). Panel data may also be limited due to measurement errors, selectivity problems, or attrition problem (Hsiao 2014; Baltagi 2008). In order to minimise these problems, it is essential that the study model is supported by established theories. That data collection is based on valid instruments to minimise the likelihood of attrition. In IB research, particularly in macroeconomic determinant studies, empirical models are analysed on economic and socio-political figures that are well established with relevant theories (Erdogan and Unver 2015; Awate et al. 2014; Zhou 2016). Drawing on extant empirical studies in developing this study model will minimise possible problems of measurement errors, selectivity problems, and/or attrition.

Generic panel data-specification model can be written as

$$y_{it} = \alpha + \beta_{1i} x_{it} + \beta_2 x_{it^{\prime}} \ldots + \beta_n x_{nit} + \varepsilon_{it}. \tag{5.1}$$

In the equation above, i is an indicator for the observation units organised into three pooled UK levels, OECD countries, and non-OECD countries; t is an indicator for time, i.e. 2009–2016; y is an indicator for *R&D* FDI for each observation unit in time t; X is an indicator for the study's predictive and control variables; and ε is an indicator for error terms. Equation (5.1) is made up of two parts: the deterministic parameters and the error term. The error term is made up of two error components, i.e., $\varepsilon_{it} = c_i + v_{it}$.

c_i is the omitted variable peculiar to each observation unit and does not change over time (e.g. geographical location, unchanging political-economic factors), while v_{it} are the idiosyncratic variables that vary across individual observation unit and overtime (i.i.d.). That is, v_{it} is usually assumed to be well behaved. If $Cov(\varepsilon_i, x_{it}) = 0$, then Eq. (5.1) can be estimated using classical OLS estimator. However, this study allows for the possibility of partial adjustment, by allowing the term y_{it} lagged 1 year as stated on the right-hand side of Eq. (5.2) accounting for the effect consistent with the agglomeration positive externalities generated by the localisation of existing R&D FDI, representing a self-reinforcing feedback effect. Hence, Eq. (5.1) is rewritten as

$$y_{it} = \alpha + \beta_0 y_{it-1} + \beta_1 + \varepsilon_{it}. \tag{5.2}$$

As shown in Eq. (5.2), a lagged dependent variable in the right-hand side of the model may cause a correlation between the lagged dependent variables with disturbance terms. Precisely, if $Cov(y_{it} - 1, \varepsilon_{it}) \neq 0$, then OLS estimation becomes inconsistent. This, therefore, requires a dynamic panel data regression model to estimate the study parameters.

Dynamic Panel Data Analysis

This study empirically examines the motivations of inward R&D FDI in the UK at the aggregate country-level, OECD, and non-OECD home countries. The choice for panel data analysis is that it allows for a more robust analysis with less potential of endogeneity problems (Baltagi 2008). This study is conducted using system generalized method of moment (sys-GMM). The preference for dynamic panel estimators over normal panel data estimators is because it's more robust to eliminate endogeneity which could result in heteroscedasticity and serial correlation (Roodman 2006; Wooldridge 2010). Adding to that, it resolves issues of endogeneity caused by lagged dependent variable as a regressor in Eq. (5.1) which could only be resolved only if T tends to be infinity (Roodman 2006). There are two generalized-method-of-moment (GMM) estimators for dynamic panel data analysis, that is, the difference GMM (diff-GMM) estimator and system GMM (sys-GMM) estimator developed by Arellano and Bond (1991), Arellano and Bover (1995), and Blundell and Bond (1998).

Employing sys-GMM estimator, as opposed to diff-GMM, is because sys-GMM estimator is more robust to eliminate endogeneity which could result in heteroscedasticity and serial correlation (Greene 2003). The sys-GMM estimator is more efficient compared to difference GMM estimator since it corrects potential bias associated with using lagged levels as instruments (Arellano and Bond 1991; Roodman 2006). With regard to data generation process, the system GMM estimators embody the below assumptions:

1. The assumption that current realisations of the dependent variable are influenced by past ones.
2. The assumption that some regressors may be predetermined but not strictly exogenous. Such that even if the regressor does not correlate

with current disturbance but still correlate with past ones. For example, the lagged dependent variable.
3. The assumption that some variables are endogenous.
4. The assumption of (within-group) individual effects such that the dependent variable consistently changes faster for some observational units than others (Blundell and Bond 1998). Another perspective to this is that the fixed effect is eliminated such that variation over time can be used to identify parameters (Arellano and Bond 1991).
5. The assumption that idiosyncratic disturbances are uncorrelated across observation units and may have individual-specific patterns of heteroscedasticity.
6. The panel is a small T and large N.
7. The assumption that instruments are internal, that is, based on lags of the instrumented variables. (Arellano and Bond 1991; Blundell and Bond 1998; Roodman 2006).

Blundell and Bond (1998) argued that using lagged levels can be a weak instrument for the regression model in differences when the explanatory variables are persistent over time. That is, if *y*it is close to a random walk. The system GMM estimator relies upon the additional moment conditions that there is no correlation between the lagged first differences of the explanatory variables used as instruments in Eq. (5.3) and the observation unit-specific effect c_i (i.e. pooled, OECD, and non-OECD) compared to the difference GMM estimator that makes use of first differencing to eliminate fixed effect in the study model and then employs lagged levels of both the dependent variable and independent variables as instruments within the dataset (Roodman 2006):

$$y_{it} = \alpha + \beta_0 y_{it} - 1 + \beta_1 x_{it} + c_i + v_{it}. \tag{5.3}$$

System GMM combines the first differences (instrumented variables) and level regressions in a system to estimate the study parameters. This is possible based on additional restrictions on the moment condition to be meant, that is:

Δy_{it-1} is a valid instrument for the variables in levels if

$$\text{cov}\left[\left(\Delta y_{it} - 1\right) * \left(c_i + v_{it}\right)\right] = 0 \quad \text{for all } i \text{ and } t. \tag{5.4}$$

Same also holds for other regressors; Δx_{it-1} is a valid instrument for the variables in levels if

$$\text{cov}\left[\left(\Delta x_{it} - 1\right) * \left(c_i + v_{it}\right)\right] = 0 \quad \text{for all } i \text{ and } t. \tag{5.5}$$

The validity of this moment condition depends on the assumption that v_{it} is not serially correlated; otherwise, the differenced instrumental variable(s) may correlate with past and contemporary errors, even with future ones as well (Cameron and Trivedi 2010).

Improving Efficiency and Diagnostic Tests

The consistency of standard GMM methodology hinges on the validity of a set of linear moment conditions. Having an endogenous variable in the study model that correlates with the error term will increase the loss of efficiency (Wooldridge 2010). Using a set of instruments in the first differenced equation or at level may not satisfy orthogonality conditions. The consistency of standard GMM methodology hinges on the validity of the above set of linear moment conditions. For this study, below are some essential tests to be performed.

Addressing Multicollinearity and Heteroscedasticity Problems

Before conducting dynamic panel data analysis, there are certain assumptions that need to be satisfied regarding issues of multicollinearity, heteroscedasticity, and endogeneity problems. Multicollinearity occurs when there is a strong correlation between two or more predictors in the regression model. There are several ways to identify multicollinearity; this could be by scanning the correlation matrix of predictor variables to detect if they correlate very highly usually above 0.80 or 0.90 (Cameron and Trivedi 2010). Another way is through the value of tolerance and variance inflation factor (VIF) value, and the rule of thumb is that the tolerance value should not be less than 0.10, while the VIF value should not be above 10 (Cameron and Trivedi 2010). For this study, the correlation matrix and VIF were conducted, and evidence from the results shows that multicollinearity does not exist.

Another key assumption is that the variance of errors is the same across all levels of the independent variables. Otherwise, when variance errors differ at a different level of independent variables, there is heteroscedasticity. In this study, evidence of heteroscedasticity is resolved with the use of VCE robust standard errors in STAT software. All model analysed are reported with robust standard errors in case of the existence of heteroscedasticity. Also, to improve the normality of the dataset, data transformation using log base 10 was done for all variables. This is consistent with previous studies that have suggested that log base 10 transformation helps to improve the normality of the data series (Kumar 2001; Falk 2014).

Endogeneity Problems

The OLS assumption of exogeneity is violated if there is a correlation between X and u. If this occurs, X is said to be an endogenous variable. The effect is that the coefficient of X in OLS regression is biased and inconsistent. Naturally, the lagged dependent variable is endogenous given that it is correlated with the error term. Thus, this test will then focus on other regressors in the study model; the aim here is to minimise the loss of efficiency due to the proliferation of instruments (Wooldridge 2010). The Hausman test principle provides a way to test whether regressors are endogenous as a consequence of comparing coefficients of different estimation methods on the same equation (usually OLS vs IV). The Hausman test comes in different versions: Durbin statistic (Durbin 1954) and Hausman statistic. If there is little difference between the OLS estimation and either IV, 2SLS, or GMM, then this concludes that the variable is exogenous and there is no need for instruments. For this study, the researcher followed this principle and did a Sargan post-estimation test to test the validity of the instrument.

Test of Over-Identification Restrictions

The Sargan test of over-identifying restrictions tests the overall relevance and validity of the instruments (Sargan 1958). Here, the null hypothesis of no misspecification is rejected if the minimised GMM criterion function registers a large value that is compared with a chi-squared distribution with the degree of freedom equals to the difference between the number of moment conditions and the number of parameters. However, it is worth noting that the Sargan statistic is not consistent in the presence of heteroscedasticity.

Hence, consideration will also be given to Hansen J statistic, which is robust in the presence of heteroscedasticity and autocorrelation (Hansen 1982). However, drawing from Roodman (2006), one major weakness of the Hansen J statistic is that it is easily biased by an increase in the number of instruments. However, one way to improve these test results is to limit the number of instruments, and as a result, it reduces the bias on the standard errors (see Calderon et al. 2002; Carkovic and Levine 2002). This procedure applies each moment condition to all available periods and reduces the over-fitting bias associated with having too many instruments.

Test for First- and Second-Order Autocorrelation

Adding to Sargan and Hansen tests for joint validity of instruments, Arellano and Bond (1991) developed this test to examine the hypothesis that the error term ε_{it} is not serially correlated. Autocorrelation of the first order is to be expected for the regression in first differences due to the construction of the differenced residuals. Thus, to check for serial correlation of order S in levels will be by looking for serial correlation of order $S + 1$ in differences (Roodman 2006). In other words, the aim is to check for first-order serial correlation in levels, and for differenced equation, the aim is to check for second-order serial correlation. However, if the test of the assumption of nonserial correlation is not satisfied, it then indicates that the instruments are bad. One way to improve or eliminate this problem is to add more lags of the dependent variable and endogenous regressors (Cameron and Trivedi 2010).

Estimating the Study Parameters

The researcher proposes to employ one-step GMM estimators for system GMM in estimating the study parameters. Using one-step GMM over two-step GMM is that it is considered more suitable for small sample size compared to two-step GMM which is considered more efficient with much larger sample size. Adding to that, all results will be reported with robust standard errors to deal with possible heteroscedasticity in the data series. This is the usual Eicker-Huber-White "sandwich" robust variance-covariance matrix for the IV estimators (Huber 1967; White 1980; Cameron and Trivedi 2010).

Conclusion

This chapter provides the necessary literature backing within the context of IB research on the chosen research design and methods employed in this study. IB research has its roots in multicultural and multidimensional fields of study that lends itself to a broad range of research designs, methodologies, and methods. The research design, methodology, and methods employed in this study are quantitative. The choice of a quantitative research approach is considered appropriate because this study seeks to examine the causal effects of the strategic and specific motivations on R&D FDI in the UK.

References

Arellano, M., & Bond, S. (1991). Some tests of specification for panel data: Monte Carlo evidence and an application to employment equations. *The Review of Economic Studies, 58*(2), 277–297.

Arellano, M., & Bover, O. (1995). Another look at the instrumental variable estimation of error-components models. *Journal of Econometrics, 68*(1), 29–51.

Awate, S., Larsen, M. M., & Mudambi, R. (2014). Accessing vs sourcing knowledge: A comparative study of R&D internationalization between emerging and advanced economy firms. *Journal of International Business Studies, 46*(1), 63–86.

Baltagi, B. (2008). *Econometric analysis of panel data*. Hoboken, NJ: John Wiley & Sons.

Birkinshaw, J. (2004). Publishing qualitative research in international business. *Handbook of Qualitative Research Methods for International Business*, pp. 570–584.

Blundell, R., & Bond, S. (1998). Initial conditions and moment restrictions in dynamic panel data models. *Journal of Econometrics, 87*(1), 115–143.

Calderon, C. A., Chong, A., & Loayza, N. V. (2002). Determinants of current account deficits in developing countries. *Contributions in Macroeconomics, 2*(1).

Cameron, A. C., & Trivedi, P. K. (2010). *Microeconometrics using stata*. College Station, TX: Stata Press.

Carkovic, M. V., & Levine, R. (2002). *Does foreign direct investment accelerate economic growth?* University of Minnesota Department of Finance Working Paper, no. 254.

Cheng, J. L., Henisz, W. J., Roth, K., & Swaminathan, A. (2009). From the Editors: Advancing interdisciplinary research in the field of international business: Prospects, issues and challenges. *Journal of International Business Studies, 40*(7), 1070–1074.

Creswell, J. W., & Creswell, J. D. (2017). *Research design: Qualitative, quantitative, and mixed methods approaches*. London: Sage Publications.

Durbin, J. (1954). Errors in variables. *Revue de l'institut International de Statistique, 22*(1/3), 23–32.

Erdogan, M., & Unver, M. (2015). Determinants of Foreign Direct Investments: Dynamic Panel Data Evidence. *International Journal of Economics and Finance, 7*(5), 82.

Fallon, G., & Cook, M. (2010). Exploring the regional distribution of inbound foreign direct investment in the UK in theory and practice: Evidence from a five-region study. *Regional Studies, 44*(3), 337–353.

Falk, M. (2014). Determinants of Greenfield Foreign Direct Investment in R&D and related activities. *FIW Research Reports Series no* . IV-002.

Greene, W. H. (2003). *Econometric analysis*. London: Pearson Education.

Hansen, L. P. (1982). Large sample properties of generalized method of moments estimators. *Econometrica: Journal of the Econometric Society, 50*(4), 1029–1054.

Hill, S., & Munday, M. (1992). The UK regional distribution of foreign direct investment: analysis and determinants. *Regional Studies, 26*(6), 535–544.

Hsiao, C. (2014). *Analysis of panel data*. Cambridge: Cambridge university press.

Huber, P. J. (1967). The behavior of maximum likelihood estimates under non-standard conditions. *Proceedings of the Fifth Berkeley Symposium on Mathematical Statistics and Probability, 1*(1), 221–233.

Hurmerinta-Peltomäki, L., & Nummela, N. (2006). Mixed methods in international business research: A value-added perspective. *Management International Review, 46*(4), 439–459.

Jones, C., & Temouri, Y. (2016). The determinants of tax haven FDI. *Journal of World Business, 51*(2), 237–250.

Kumar, N. (2001). Determinants of location of overseas R&D activity of multinational enterprises: the case of US and Japanese corporations. *Research Policy, 30*(1), 159–174.

Oppermann, M. (2000). Triangulation—A methodological discussion. *International Journal of Tourism Research, 2*(2), 141–145.

Popkewitz, T. S. (2012). *Paradigm and Ideology in Educational Research (RLE Edu L): The Social Functions of the Intellectual.* London: Routledge.

Quinlan, C., Babin, B., Carr, J., & Griffin, M. (2019). *Business research methods.* Andover: South Western Cengage.

Roodman, D. (2006). *How to do xtabond2: An introduction to difference and system GMM in Stata.* Center for Global Development working paper, No. 103.

Sargan, J. D. (1958). The estimation of economic relationships using instrumental variables. *Econometrica: Journal of the Econometric Society, 26*(3), 393–415.

Scandura, T. A., & Williams, E. A. (2000). Research methodology in management: Current practices, trends, and implications for future research. *Academy of Management Journal, 43*(6), 1248–1264.

Soiferman, L. K. (2010). *Compare and contrast inductive and deductive research approaches.* University of Manitoba working paper, No. 10.

Teddlie, C., & Tashakkori, A. (2003). Major issues and controversies in the use of mixed methods in the social and behavioral sciences. *Handbook of Mixed Methods in Social & Behavioral Research, 1*, 3–50.

Tuli, F. (2010). The basis of distinction between qualitative and quantitative research in social science: Reflection on ontological, epistemological and methodological perspectives. *Ethiopian Journal of Education and Sciences, 6*(1), 33–42.

Welch, D., & Welch, L. (2004). *Getting published: The last great hurdle?* Cheltenham: Edward Elgar Publishing.

White, H. (1980). A heteroskedasticity-consistent covariance matrix estimator and a direct test for heteroskedasticity. *Econometrica: Journal of the Econometric Society, 48*(4), 817–838.

Wooldridge, J. M. (2010). *Econometric analysis of cross section and panel data.* Cambridge: MIT press.

Zhou, Y. (2016). Drivers of Globalization of R&D Investment by US Multinational Enterprises: Evidence from Industry-Level Data. *International Journal of Economics and Finance, 8*(2), 51–69.

6

Motivations of R&D FDI in the UK: Analysis, Discussion, and Conclusion

Abstract The purpose of this chapter is to carry out an empirical analysis of the specific and strategic motivations of R&D FDI in the UK. In this chapter, the study investigates R&D FDI motivations considering the heterogeneity in the economic and technological capability of the investing MNEs from home countries grouped into OECD and non-OECD countries. This approach allows for easy comparison of results to provide greater insight into the similarity and dissimilarity of motivations among MNEs engaged in R&D FDI in the UK. The study extends MNE internationalisation literature by providing empirical evidence on different strategies and the specific motivations of R&D FDI in the UK.

Keywords Exploitation • Augmentation • Market • Efficiency • Strategic • Assets

The Study Model and Variables Specification

As depicted in the study analytical framework in Fig. 4.1, this study provides empirical evidence based on a complementary set of hypotheses which provide a structural approach in modelling the strategic and specific

O. Igbinigie et al., *Strategic Motivations of Inward R&D FDI*,
https://doi.org/10.1007/978-3-030-41015-5_6

motivations of R&D FDI between heterogeneous home country groups in the UK (i.e. OECD vs non-OECD countries). The model on the strategic and specific motivations of R&D FDI is structured as follows:

$$\begin{aligned} R\,\&\,DFDI_{it} = \alpha &+ \beta_1 \text{Market} - \text{seeking}_{it} + \beta_2 \text{Efficiency} \\ &- \text{seeking}_{it} + \beta_3 \text{ Strategic Asset} - \text{seeking}_{it} \\ &+ \beta_n \text{Control variables}_{itn} + \varepsilon_{it}. \end{aligned} \tag{6.1}$$

From Eq. (6.1), *R&Dfdi* represents the R&D expenditure performed by foreign MNEs in the UK. *i* in the model represents the total R&D expenditure performed by a particular MNE at time *t*. *i* and *t* data series will be the UK as a whole, then grouped into OECD, and non-OECD countries in three separate models, while εit is an indicator of the error term. Table 6.1 shows the study variables and proxies with the expected signs and the units of analysis. All proxies used are made in relative terms to the UK to derive the study panel dataset.

Table 6.1 shows the study variables and proxies with the expected signs and the units of analysis. All proxies used are made in relative terms to the UK's to derive the study panel dataset. Below are further discussions justifying the choice of the chosen variables in Table 6.1.

The Dependent Variables

The choice of R&D expenditure as the dependent variable is consistent with prior empirical studies, for example, Veliyath and Sambharya (2011) used R&D expenditures (in a million of PPP dollars) of MNEs' foreign affiliates as a proxy for international R&D investment flows. Wang (2010) used a measure of R&D expenditures to GDP (i.e. R&D intensity) to examine 26 OECD countries. Some other studies have also used count variables of projects executed or jobs created (e.g. Falk 2014; Antonietti and Cainelli 2008). As pointed out in Hill and Munday (1992), measuring FDI using new projects may not be suitable for this study. This is because projects do not differentiate between new projects and expansionary projects and, also, it tends to ignore variation in values.

Table 6.1 Operationalisation of variables and expected results

Variables	Proxy	Expected results	Unit of analysis
R&D FDI	R&D expenditures by MNEs	Dependent Variable	The ratio of home countries' R&D expenditures in the UK to the UK total
Market-seeking	GDP	Positive	The ratio of home countries' GDP to the UK's
Efficiency-seeking	R&D personnel	Positive	The ratio of home countries' number of R&D personnel to the UK's
Strategic asset-seeking	Patent intensity (patent application divided by population)	Positive	The ratio of home countries' patent intensity to the UK's
Self-reinforcing effects	Lagged R&D FDI (−1)	Positive	1 year lagged of R&D FDI
Trade openness	Import plus export	Positive	The ratio of home countries' trade openness to the UK's
Interest rate	Interest rate percentage (%)	Negative	The ratio of home countries' interest rate to the UK's

In the same vein, when new jobs created are used, it may lead to more problems, especially difficulty in determining the actual jobs created or job safeguarded. Fallon and Cook (2010) added that there is still a problem of determining the actual job lost or displaced as a result of the new job created. For this study, the dependent variable dataset was obtained from the FAME database.

The Predictive Variables

The study examines three main specific motivations, that is, market-seeking, efficiency-seeking, and strategic asset-seeking, by which complementary set of hypotheses were developed to model R&D FDI strategic motivations (based on asset exploitation and asset augmentation). In Eq. (6.1), the first predictive variable will proxy for market-seeking motivations; however, Billington (1999) noted that there is no catch-all variable for market-seeking. MNEs' R&D subsidiaries are located in foreign locations with high market potential either for adaptive R&D (asset exploitation) or to cover the cost of R&D to develop new knowledge or learn to create new knowledge (asset augmentation). The UK is attractive to market-seeking R&D FDI either for adaptive or market gains. The market-seeking motivation in the study model will be represented by GDP obtained from the World Bank's World Development Indicators.

To proxy for efficiency-seeking, this study employs the quality of human capital proxied by R&D personnel. The choice of the human capital proxy rather than labour cost as a measure of efficiency-seeking motivation is in line with other previous studies like Awate et al. (2014) and Zhou (2016). These authors support the argument that the quality of human capital is favoured over labour cost based on the fact that MNEs' R&D FDI is attracted to locations with higher human capital quality than labour cost. Efficiency-seeking R&D FDI that seeks economies of scale and scope could also be achieved through human capital in order to gain operational flexibility. Here, authors argued that efficiency-seeking allows MNEs to concentrate on its core competencies in pre-existing assets (Awate et al. 2014; Zhou 2016). In this study, efficiency-seeking is considered to depend on how well the host location meets the human capital requirements of foreign firms' R&D FDI activities. In R&D FDI literature, there is weak evidence that differences in the cost of R&D personnel are a major driver for the internationalisation of R&D. Nonetheless, wage differences gain importance when firms consider locating innovative activities in emerging and developing economies (Thursby and Thursby 2006). In the case of advanced economies, R&D FDI activities may largely depend on how well the location meets the human capital requirements of foreign firms.

To proxy for strategic asset-seeking R&D FDI, the study employs patent intensity (measured by patent applications divided by population obtained from the World Bank's World Development Indicators). Strategic assets relate to specific scientific and technological expertise present in a host location. This could be as a result of national innovation system captured by the scale of national technological efforts or key research institutions (Kuemmerle 1999; Von Zedtwitz and Gassmann 2002; Cantwell and Mudambi 2005). The choice of patent intensity is to capture how highly innovative-related FDI like R&D is attracted due to scientific and technological efforts produced through patent applications in the UK. The search for strategic assets amplifies the need to locate R&D FDI in well-chosen countries or regions that are more innovative and technologically advanced (Kuemmerle 1999; Dunning 1998). Access to R&D resources and localised knowledge appears to be the dominant motivation for R&D investment in developed countries (Odagiri and Yasuda 1996; Iwasa and Odagiri 2004; Chung and Yeaple 2008).

To examine the strategic motivations of assets-exploiting and assets-augmenting and its different specific motives, the study examines the interactions of the specific motivations between OECD and non-OECD home countries. This research proposes that MNEs engaging in R&D FDI from advanced industrial and highly technological countries (e.g. OECD countries) will then undertake both asset-exploiting and asset-augmenting activities, while MNEs from less industrial and technological countries will then undertake asset-augmenting R&D activities. Drawing from Cantwell and Mudambi (2005), Awate et al. (2014), and Denicolai et al. (2014), it is suggested that MNEs with pre-existing firm-specific advantages have a higher level of R&D FDI. For this study, it is expected that the empirical results for OECD countries' specific motivations will have a higher magnitude compared to non-OECD countries. The idea here is that the quality of the host location in research would influence the extent foreign R&D affiliates exploit existing firm-specific advantages, and/or build up new firm-specific advantages (Kuemmerle 1999). As suggested in Criscuolo et al. (2005), given that products are usually multi-technology based, MNEs that engage in both strategies in same host location will tend to exchange information between both types of R&D activities.

The Control Variables

The predictive effect of the empirical analysis is supported with some control variables. Those variables that could also influence the model include self-reinforcing effect (proxied by R&D FDI lagged 1 year), trade (proxied by the sum of import and export), tax rate (proxied by corporation tax), exchange rate (proxied by real effective exchange rate index 2010 = 100), and interest rate (proxied by real interest rate %). The choice of R&D expenditure lagged 1 year as part of the control variables is to allow for the possibility of partial adjustment and to account for the effect consistent with positive externalities generated by the localisation of existing R&D FDI. This represents a self-reinforcing feedback effect consistent with existing FDI empirical studies; for example, see Jensen et al. (2007) and Zheng (2011). After controlling for the effect of self-reinforcing effects, trade openness (proxied by the sum of import and export) will be included as a control variable. The level of trade openness indicates the degree of comparative advantage of the host country and, thus, can guarantee a higher return on investments through lower transaction costs (Dunning 1998).

Similarly, the rate of corporation tax is an effective policy instrument to facilitate FDI inflows. According to Blonigen (2005), the effects of corporation tax on FDI vary substantially depending on the tax treatment in the host and home country, and the FDI activities involved. Adding to that, the relationship between host country exchange rate and that of the home country could influence FDI inflows (Mody and Srinivasan 1991; Buckley et al. 2007). Another economic variable that attracts FDI inflows is interest rates. As a proxy to control for the precariousness of economic atmosphere, interest rates reflect the volatility of the host economic position for investments.

Data Analysis

This section provides details of the descriptive statistics and analytical statistics. All dataset used are made in relative terms (i.e. making the UK as the denominator). The UK total (labelled as UK pooled) represents the dataset obtained for all 36 countries for 8 years amounting to 288 observations. OECD countries include 25 countries for the same period amounting to 200 observations, while non-OECD countries include 11 countries for the same period amounting to 88 observations.

Descriptive Statistics

Table 6.2 presents the descriptive statistics showing key features of the study dataset grouped into UK-pooled, OECD, and non-OECD countries. With the UK-pooled average of 3.7%, OECD countries have a higher-average R&D FDI expenditure of 5%, and non-OECD countries 0.8%. This implies that the UK received more R&D FDI from MNEs from OECD countries compared to non-OECD countries. Regarding the main predictive variables for the study, similar patterns were observed: FDI motivations (proxied by GDP, number of R&D personnel, patent

Table 6.2 Summary of descriptive statistics

Variable	Obs	Mean	Std. dev.	Min	Max
UK pooled					
R&D FDI	288	0.037096	0.136011	0.000029	1.402384
Mkt	288	0.609582	1.145554	0.0054	7.0905
Efficiency	288	0.783796	0.420248	0.02892	1.974478
Stra-assets	288	1.287588	2.407514	0.003219	14.3813
Trade	288	1.880762	1.464885	0.378272	7.777213
Tax	288	0.684668	0.295812	0.002279	1.476067
ExRate	288	0.910407	0.109698	0.575737	1.175498
IntRate	288	−2.33145	5.530627	−38.398	16.17282
OECD countries					
R&D FDI	200	0.049883	0.161429	0.000029	1.402384
Mkt	200	0.648885	1.229257	0.0054	7.0905
Efficiency	200	0.899114	0.401703	0.061915	1.974478
Stra-assets	200	1.632749	2.789322	0.022572	14.3813
Trade	200	1.547037	0.75323	0.440771	3.867548
Tax	200	0.777197	0.253135	0.325995	1.476067
ExRate	200	0.919717	0.10129	0.575737	1.175498
IntRate	200	−1.92942	2.861813	−11.3528	5.696894
Non-OECD countries					
R&D FDI	88	0.008034	0.013712	0.000039	0.068598
Mkt	88	0.520257	0.927944	0.0097	4.2763
Efficiency	88	0.521709	0.336829	0.02892	1.355585
Stra-assets	88	0.50313	0.65411	0.003219	3.09704
Trade	88	2.639229	2.223354	0.378272	7.777213
Tax	88	0.474374	0.278717	0.002279	1.075742
ExRate	88	0.889249	0.12481	0.601669	1.132483
IntRate	88	−3.24516	8.997516	−38.398	16.17282

intensity) are compared to the UK pool of 61%, 78.4%, and 129%. OECD countries are higher with 64.9%, 90%, and 163%, while non-OECD countries have 52%, 52.2%, and 50.3%, respectively.

Pre-estimation Tests

The summary results in Table 6.3 correlation matrix and Table 6.4 tolerance and variance inflation factor (VIF) value indicate that multicollinearity does not exist in the study variables. Multicollinearity exists if the study variables correlate very highly usually above 0.80 or 0.90 or the tolerance values should not be less than 0.10 and VIF value not above 10 (Cameron and Trivedi 2010). Also, in this study, there is evidence of heteroscedasticity, and one way to solve it is to use the VCE robust standard errors in STATA software. All models analysed are reported with robust standard errors in case of the existence of heteroscedasticity (in STATA this is done with the command "VCE (robust)"). Also, to improve the normality of the dataset, data transformation using log base 10 was done in all the variables. This is consistent with previous studies that have suggested that log base 10 transformation helps to improve the normality of the data series (Kumar 2001; Falk 2014).

Empirical Results of System GMM Estimation

Table 6.5 presents the empirical results of the study dynamic panel data analysis using system GMM (sys-GMM) developed by Blundell and Bond (1998). The study used one-step GMM estimator to analyse the parameters. The choice of one-step GMM over two-step GMM is considered more suitable for small sample size compared to two-step GMM which is considered more efficient with much larger sample size (Arellano and Bond 1991).

Models I, II, and III reveal that R&D FDI in the UK is for market-seeking, efficiency-seeking, and strategic assets-seeking motivations, thus providing empirical support for the study Hypotheses H1, H2, and H3. In terms of H4, H4a, and H4b, the interaction of empirical results found for OECD and non-OECD country groups as exhibited in Models II

Table 6.3 Summary of correlation matrix

	Lnrdfdi	Market	Efficiency	Stra-assets	lnTrade	lnTax	lnExRate	lnintRate
Lnrdfdi	1							
Market	0.5251***	1						
	0.0051							
Efficiency	0.2540****	0.0915	1					
	0.0287	0.1214						
Stra-assets	0.0905	0.0386	0.1777***	1				
	0.1256	0.5141	0.0025					
lnTrade	0.2075***	−0.1819***	0.0855	−0.1864	1			
	0.0004	0.0019	0.1477	0.0015				
lnTax	−0.1282	0.3025	−0.1485	−0.0981	−0.4210**	1		
	0.0297	0.5238	0.0116	0.0967	0.047			
lnExRate	−0.0586	−0.0492	−0.1290***	0.0416	0.0886	−0.2506*	1	
	0.3215	0.4054	0.0285	0.4815	0.1336	0.081		
lnintRate	−0.1672*	−0.1067	−0.1505*	−0.0545	−0.0843	0.0403	0.1324*	1
	0.0753	0.8742	0.0875	0.7456	0.1356	0.4897	0.0602	

Note: $^{*}p < 0.10$; $^{**}p < 0.05$; $^{***}p < 0.01$

Table 6.4 Summary of tolerance and variance inflation factors

Variable	VIF	1/VIF
Market	1.48	0.67544
Efficiency	1.33	0.75105
Stra-assets	1.16	0.86278
lnTrade	1.13	0.88269
lnTax	1.11	0.9003
lnExRate	1.1	0.91031
lnintRate	1.09	0.92012
Mean VIF	1.2	

Table 6.5 Summary result of system GMM estimation

Models	(I)	(II)	(III)
	Pooled	OECD	Non-OECD
Market	0.3246***	0.3324***	0.1270***
	0.005	0.001	0.004
Efficiency	0.0984*	0.1651**	0.0326
	0.090	0.046	0.168
Stra-assets	0.0922**	0.1715***	0.0512*
	0.002	0.007	0.065
R&Dfd$_{i-1}$	0.8046***	0.7145***	0.8517***
	0.000	0.000	0.000
lnTrade	0.6239**	0.8333***	0.4860**
	0.030	0.000	0.034
lnCorp.Tax	−1.1172	−0.9201	−0.6259*
	0.120	0.102	0.081
lnExRate	0.8097*	1.1677**	0.5009
	0.097	0.041	0.116
lnintRate	−0.1243	−0.2792*	−0.08583
	0.426	0.076	0.255
Wald test	650.31	639.71	741.91
Prob. > Chi^2	0.000	0.000	0.0000
No. Obs.	252	175	77
No. of groups	36	25	11
AR1	−3.9706	−3.646	−2.0829
P-value	0.000	0.003	0.0373
AR2	−0.72427	−1.2186	0.67358
P-value	0.4689	0.2230	0.5006
Sargan Chi^2	196.763	203.8991	87.8800
P-value	0.7012	0.1100	0.8209

Note: $^{*}p < 0.10$; $^{**}p < 0.05$; $^{***}p < 0.01$

and III shows different strategic motivations for asset-exploiting and asset-augmenting activities which provide empirical support for H4. For OECD countries, R&D FDI has a higher magnitude for market-seeking, efficiency-seeking, and strategic asset-seeking motivations which provide support for H4a asset-exploiting and asset-augmenting strategies, whereas for non-OECD countries, R&D FDI is for market-seeking and strategic asset-seeking which provide support for H4b asset-augmenting strategies.

Discussion of Findings

Consistent with the study hypotheses, the empirical analysis revealed that market-seeking, efficiency-seeking, and strategic asset-seeking motivations are significant positive determinants of R&D FDI in the UK. This is, therefore, consistent with the economic theory of FDI motivations proposed by Dunning (1979, 1988, 2009). For example, the significant positive results found for market-seeking motivation for the UK-pooled, OECD, and non-OECD countries draw support from extant empirical literature: Kumar (2001), Athukorala and Kohpaiboon (2010), Belderbos et al. (2014), and Falk (2014). These authors provide empirical evidence which indicated that locations with high income (or with potentials for high-income growth) attract R&D FDI. Market-seeking R&D FDI permits economies of scale through product and process adaptation to exploit the host location local resources and production conditions, such that the MNEs find it easier to cover the cost of R&D activity (Cantwell and Mudambi 2005). A higher coefficient estimate for market-seeking on R&D FDI for OECD countries indicates that countries with high per capita income and technological capabilities are more influenced by market-seeking motivation compared to countries with low per capita income and technological capabilities. This, therefore, suggests that MNEs from OECD countries with high technological capabilities and with pre-existing home-based competences are more attracted for market-seeking motivation than non-OECD countries. As revealed in Dunning and Narula (1995) and Falk (2014), MNEs established foreign R&D units to adapt their products to specific local markets, thereby taken advantage of market opportunities in the host location. The central idea here is that

R&D foreign affiliates are designed to exploit existing technological capability developed by the parent firm to support the host market conditions and cover the cost of foreign R&D.

The empirical results show that R&D FDI for UK country-level and OECD group are attracted by efficiency-seeking motivation (proxied by R&D personnel). The empirical result also indicates that the UK's inward R&D FDI from non-OECD countries are not attracted to efficiency-seeking motivation. A possible explanation for the significant result found for OECD countries' group and insignificant result for non-OECD countries' group for efficiency-seeking R&D FDI is consistent with extant literatures that argued that new products are multi-technology based and that firms with pre-existing capabilities would engage in both asset-augmenting and asset-exploiting strategies with a view to sustaining technology leadership (Bardhan 2006; Fifarek and Veloso 2010; Nieto and Rodríguez 2011; Awate et al. 2014; Zhou 2016). The idea here is that MNEs with pre-existing home-based competences will establish foreign R&D unit to allow the firms to focus on their core capabilities, for greater organisational flexibility and efficiency. Kuemmerle (1999) noted that, when considering opening an R&D lab abroad, MNEs favour host locations with outstanding researchers and graduate students. Bardhan (2006) and Stephan and Silvia (2008) revealed that MNEs' R&D internationalisation in search of human capital is to gain greater efficiency. Kinkel and Maloca (2008) showed that capacity bottlenecks are the most frequent reason why German firms move R&D to foreign locations. Lewin et al. (2009) revealed that the shortage of highly skilled science and engineering talents partially explains the relocation of product development from the US to other parts of the world.

The empirical results show that R&D FDI is attracted for strategic asset-seeking motivations (proxied by patent intensity) for all the models (pooled-level, OECD, and non-OECD groups). These results corroborate with Von Zedtwitz and Gassmann (2002), Iwasa and Odagiri (2004), and Di Minin et al. (2012) who argued that MNEs established R&D units abroad to gain access to crucial inputs such as new knowledge and technology that are location specific and are not easily available in their principal or home markets. Another explanation for this result is that firms from home countries with advanced technological capabilities may engage in both asset-augmenting and asset-exploiting activities to sustain technology leadership, while firms from home countries with less technological capabilities may tend to seek new knowledge for catch-up (asset-augmenting). These suggest that the strength of the location in science would influence the extent foreign affiliates to exploit existing firm-specific advantages and build up new firm-specific advantages or instead learn new knowledge to catch up and get on par with industry leaders (Kuemmerle 1996, 1999; Awate et al. 2014).

In terms of control variables, the positive coefficients reported for self-reinforcing effects of R&D FDI are consistent with findings reported in Agiomirgianakis et al. (2003) and Zheng (2011) who adopted a similar measure of FDI self-reinforcing effects and reported positive results. These results imply that positive externalities from previous FDIs are an indication of the present condition and the future prospects of the host location (in this case, the UK). Self-reinforcing effects also reflect the concentration of economic activities that give rise to economies of scale and positive externalities. Cantwell and Piscitello (2002) and Chung and Alcácer (2002) argued that the presence of inter-organisational knowledge due to the pool of specialised activities could improve innovative performance. Belderbos et al. (2014) noted that by undertaking R&D activity in technology clusters, firms get access to field-specific knowledge and can improve the productivity of their R&D activities. Likewise, trade openness is significant for the pooled UK country level and the disaggregated groups (OECD and non-OECD countries). The positive coefficients reported for trade openness corroborate with studies like Grossman and Helpman (1991), Raines and Brown (1999), and Yang et al. (2019). Grossman and Helpman (1991) proposed that trade liberalisation promotes competition among firms and thus provides incentives for technological innovation like R&D activities. Raines and Brown (1999) documented that UK's success in attracting FDI is anchored on its liberalisation policies towards encouraging foreign investors, paralleled with a robust privatisation programme in key sectors like railways, telecommunication, water, electricity, and financial deregulation.

On the effect of corporation tax, the empirical results show that high corporation tax has a negative influence on non-OECD countries' R&D FDI only, but insignificant results have been seen for pooled and OECD countries. The insignificant results reported for the UK as a whole and OECD countries compared to the significant results found for non-OECD countries corroborate with Bénassy-Quéré et al. (2007). They revealed that FDI by MNEs from high-income countries to similar countries typically do not think highly of the statutory tax rate to be a major influence on FDI among other FDI determinants. In contrast, MNEs from non-OECD countries with different tax policies (usually with weaker tax regime/system in their home countries) will consider taxation like every other important determinant of FDI flows.

The empirical result shows that exchange rates have significant positive effects on the UK-pooled and OECD countries but insignificant results for non-OECD countries. These corroborate with Froot and Stein (1989), who recorded that the appreciation of home currency increases MNCs' wealth position reducing the relative cost of capital and then invests actively in foreign markets. Yol and Teng (2012) found that the real appreciation of the Malaysian currency is associated with FDI inflows into Malaysia, while Nyarko and Barnor (2011) also reported a positive but insignificant relationship between exchange rate and FDI inflows into Ghana. Lastly, interest rate's negative influence on R&D FDI in all observations but significant for OECD countries' group only draw support from studies like Yang et al. (2019) who investigated the determinants of FDI in Australia and found that high interest rates are negatively significant with FDI in the 1980s and early 1990s. Buckley et al. (2007) noted that volatile and unpredictable interest rates in a host country discourage market-seeking FDI by creating uncertainty and by making long-term corporate planning problematic, especially in respect of price-setting and profit expectations.

In summary, from the empirical analysis, the results show that R&D FDI in the UK is for market-seeking, efficiency-seeking, and strategic asset-seeking motivations, thus providing empirical support for the study hypotheses. Also, revealed is that different home countries' groups follow differing strategic and specific motivations in their R&D FDI in the UK. The findings suggest that R&D FDI by OECD countries are influenced by market-seeking, efficiency-seeking, and strategic asset-seeking motivations which corroborate with the hypothesis that such MNEs with home-based assets usually combine both asset-exploiting and asset-augmenting strategies to gain complementary assets in the host location considered as a centre of excellence. When compared to the non-OECD countries' group, only market-seeking and strategic asset-seeking motivations are relevant, hence supporting asset-augmenting strategy.

Conclusion

This chapter reported empirical analysis of the specific and strategic motivations of R&D FDI in the UK. The study investigated R&D FDI motivations considering heterogeneity in the economic and technological capability of the investing MNEs, based on their home countries and grouped into OECD and non-OECD countries. The empirical analysis showed that R&D FDI in the UK is for market-seeking, efficiency-seeking, and strategic asset-seeking motivations, thus providing empirical support for the study hypotheses. The different home country groups followed differing strategic and specific motivations in their R&D FDI in the UK. The findings suggest that R&D FDI by OECD countries is affected by market-seeking, efficiency-seeking, and strategic asset-seeking motivations which corroborate the hypothesis that MNEs with home-based assets usually combine both asset-exploiting and asset-augmenting strategies to gain complementary assets in the host location, which is considered a centre of excellence. When compared to the non-OECD country group, only market-seeking and strategic asset-seeking motivations were relevant, thus supporting an asset-augmenting strategy.

References

Agiomirgianakis, G. M., Asteriou, D., & Papathoma, K. (2003). *The determinants of foreign direct investment: A panel data study for the OECD countries.* City University London, Discussion Paper Series, no. 03/06.

Antonietti, R., & Cainelli, G. (2008). Spatial agglomeration, technology and outsourcing of knowledge-intensive business services: Empirical insights from Italy. *International Journal of Services Technology and Management, 10*(2–4), 273–298.

Arellano, M., & Bond, S. (1991). Some tests of specification for panel data: Monte Carlo evidence and an application to employment equations. *The Review of Economic Studies, 58*(2), 277–297.
Athukorala, P., & Kohpaiboon, A. (2010). Globalization of R&D by US-based multinational enterprises. *Research Policy, 39*(10), 1335–1347.
Awate, S., Larsen, M. M. and Mudambi, R. (2014). Accessing vs sourcing knowledge: A comparative study of R&D internationalization between emerging and advanced economy firms. *Journal of International Business Studies, 46*(1), 63–86.
Bardhan, A. D. (2006). Managing globalization of R&D: Organizing for off-shoring innovation. *Human Systems Management, 25*(2), 103–114.
Belderbos, R., Van Roy, V., Leten, B., & Thijs, B. (2014). Academic research strengths and multinational firms' foreign R&D location decisions: Evidence from R&D investments in European regions. *Environment and Planning A, 46*(4), 920–942.
Bénassy-Quéré, A., Coupet, M., & Mayer, T. (2007). Institutional determinants of foreign direct investment. *The World Economy, 30*(5), 764–782.
Billington, N. (1999). The location of foreign direct investment: An empirical analysis. *Applied Economics, 31*(1), 65–76.
Blonigen, B. A. (2005). A review of the empirical literature on FDI determinants. *Atlantic Economic Journal, 33*(4), 383–403.
Blundell, R., & Bond, S. (1998). Initial conditions and moment restrictions in dynamic panel data models. *Journal of Econometrics, 87*(1), 115–143.
Buckley, P. J., Clegg, L. J., Cross, A. R., Liu, X., Voss, H., & Zheng, P. (2007). The determinants of Chinese outward foreign direct investment. *Journal of International Business Studies, 38*(4), 499–518.
Cameron, A. C., & Trivedi, P. K. (2010). *Microeconometrics using stata.* College Station, TX: Stata press.
Cantwell, J., & Mudambi, R. (2005). MNE competence-creating subsidiary mandates. *Strategic Management Journal, 26*(12), 1109–1128.
Cantwell, J., & Piscitello, L. (2002). The location of technological activities of MNCs in European regions: The role of spillovers and local competencies. *Journal of International Management, 8*(1), 69–96.
Chung, W., & Alcácer, J. (2002). Knowledge seeking and location choice of foreign direct investment in the United States. *Management Science, 48*(12), 1534–1554.
Chung, W., & Yeaple, S. (2008). International knowledge sourcing: Evidence from US firms expanding abroad. *Strategic Management Journal, 29*(11), 1207–1224.

Criscuolo, P., Narula, R. and Verspagen, B. (2005). Role of home and host country innovation systems in R&D internationalisation: a patent citation analysis. *Economics of Innovation and New Technology, 14*(5), 417–433.

Denicolai, S., Zucchella, A., & Strange, R. (2014). Knowledge assets and firm international performance. *International Business Review, 23*(1), 55–62.

Di Minin, A., Zhang, J., & Gammeltoft, P. (2012). Chinese foreign direct investment in R&D in Europe: A new model of R&D internationalization? *European Management Journal, 30*(3), 189–203.

Dunning, J. H. (1979) Explaining Changing Patterns of International Production: In Defence of the Eclectic Theory: Explaining Changing Patterns of International Production. *Oxford Bulletin of Economics and Statistics, 41*(4), 269–295.

Dunning, J. H. (1988). The eclectic paradigm of international production: A restatement and some possible extensions. *Journal of International Business Studies, 4*(7), 1–31.

Dunning, J. H. (1998). Location and the multinational enterprise: A neglected factor? *Journal of International Business Studies, 1*(3), 45–66.

Dunning, J. H. (2009). Location and the multinational enterprise: John Dunning's thoughts on receiving the journal of international business studies 2008 decade award. *Journal of International Business Studies, 40*(1), 20–34.

Dunning, J. H., & Narula, R. (1995). The R&D activities of foreign firms in the United States. *International Studies of Management & Organization, 25*(1–2), 39–74.

Falk, M. (2014). *Determinants of Greenfield Foreign Direct Investment in R&D and related activities.* FIW Research Reports Series no. IV-002.

Fallon, G., & Cook, M. (2010). Exploring the regional distribution of inbound foreign direct investment in the UK in theory and practice: Evidence from a five-region study. *Regional Studies, 44*(3), 337–353.

Fifarek, B. J., & Veloso, F. M. (2010). Offshoring and the global geography of innovation. *Journal of Economic Geography, 10*(4), 559–578.

Froot, K. A. and Stein, J. C. (1989). Exchange rates and foreign direct investment: an imperfect capital markets approach. *The quarterly journal of economics, 106* (4), 1191–1217.

Grossman, G., & Helpman, E. (1991). *Innovation and growth in the global economy.* Cambridge: MIT press.

Hill, S., & Munday, M. (1992). The UK regional distribution of foreign direct investment: Analysis and determinants. *Regional Studies, 26*(6), 535–544.

Iwasa, T., & Odagiri, H. (2004). Overseas R&D, knowledge sourcing, and patenting: An empirical study of Japanese R&D investment in the US. *Research Policy, 33*(5), 807–828.

Jensen, J., Rutherford, T., & Tarr, D. (2007). The impact of liberalizing barriers to foreign direct investment in services: The case of Russian accession to the World Trade Organization. *Review of Development Economics, 11*(3), 482–506.

Kinkel, S., & Maloca, S. (2008). R & D relocation overseas sales of German development. *Journal of Purchasing and Supply Management, 15*(3), 154–165.

Kuemmerle, W. (1996). Home base and foreign direct investment in R&D. Ph.D. Thesis: Harvard Business School.

Kuemmerle, W. (1999). Foreign direct investment in industrial research in the pharmaceutical and electronics industries-results from a survey of multinational firms. *Research Policy, 28*(2), 179–193.

Kumar, N. (2001). Determinants of location of overseas R&D activity of multinational enterprises: The case of US and Japanese corporations. *Research Policy, 30*(1), 159–174.

Lewin, A. Y., Massini, S., & Peeters, C. (2009). Why are companies offshoring innovation? the emerging global race for talent. *Journal of International Business Studies, 40*(6), 901–925.

Mody, A., & Srinivasan, K. (1991). Japanese and US firms as foreign investors: Do they march to the same tune? *Canadian Journal of Economics, 31* (4), 778–799.

Nieto, M. J., & Rodríguez, A. (2011). Offshoring of R&D: Looking abroad to improve innovation performance. *Journal of International Business Studies, 42*(3), 345–361.

Nyarko, P. A., & Barnor, C. (2011). Effects of exchange rate regimes on FDI inflows in Ghana. *International Journal of Economics and Finance, 3*(3), 277–281.

Odagiri, H., & Yasuda, H. (1996). The determinants of overseas R&D by Japanese firms: An empirical study at the industry and company levels. *Research Policy, 25*(7), 1059–1079.

Raines, P., & Brown, R. (1999). *Policy competition and foreign direct investment in Europe*. London: Ashgate Publication Limited.

Stephan, M., & Silvia, M. (2008). A dynamic perspective on next-generation offshoring: The global sourcing of science and engineering talent. *The Academy of Management Perspectives, 22*(3), 35–54.

Thursby, J. G., & Thursby, M. C. (2006). *Here or there? A survey of factors in multinational R&D location: Report to the government/university/industry research roundtable*. Washington, DC: National Academies Press.

Veliyath, R. and Sambharya, R. B. (2011). R&D investments of multinational corporations. *Management International Review, 51*(3), 407–428.

Von Zedtwitz, M., & Gassmann, O. (2002). Market versus technology drive in R&D internationalization: Four different patterns of managing research and development. *Research Policy, 31*(4), 569–588.

Wang, E. C. (2010). Determinants of R&D investment: The extreme-bounds-analysis approach applied to 26 OECD countries. *Research Policy, 39*(1), 103–116.

Yang, C., Matsuura, T., & Ito, T. (2019). R&D and patenting activities of foreign firms in China: The case of Japan. *Japan and the World Economy, 49*, 151–160.

Yol, M. A., & Teng, N. T. (2012). Estimating the domestic determinants of foreign direct investment flows in Malaysia: Evidence from cointegration and error-correction model. *Jurnal Pengurusan, 28*(2009), 3–22.

Zheng, P. (2011). The determinants of disparities in inward FDI flows to the three macro-regions of China. *Post-Communist Economies, 23*(02), 257–270.

Zhou, Y. (2016). Drivers of globalization of R&D investment by US multinational enterprises: Evidence from industry-level data. *International Journal of Economics and Finance, 8*(2), 51–69.

7

Research Conclusions and Emerging Agenda

Abstract This research investigates the motivations of R&D FDI. This study was motivated by the need to provide empirical evidence on a less-researched aspect of FDI, that is, R&D FDI. This study recognised R&D FDI to be similar to other traditional elements of FDI (e.g. production) and thus hypothesised that inward R&D FDI in the UK is attracted by specific motivations for market-seeking, efficiency-seeking, and strategic asset-seeking motivations. And that the specific motivations by heterogeneous investing MNE (OECD vs non-OECD) would explain the strategic motivations of inward R&D FDI in the UK. This chapter concludes this study by providing a conclusion summarising the study empirical findings, outlining its contributions to knowledge and practice. This chapter also makes salient recommendations for future research and identified some limitations experienced in undertaking this study.

Keywords Exploitation • Augmentation • Market • Efficiency • Strategic • Assets

O. Igbinigie et al., *Strategic Motivations of Inward R&D FDI*,
https://doi.org/10.1007/978-3-030-41015-5_7

Introduction

This research investigates R&D FDI's motivations in the UK. This research was motivated by the need to provide empirical evidence in a less-researched functional aspect of FDI, that is, R&D FDI. The study covers 36 home countries for a period of 8 years (2009–2016). The study datasets were organised to examine the UK as a whole (pooled UK level) and grouped into OECD and non-OECD countries. The OECD countries comprise 25 countries, and the non-OECD countries comprise 11 countries. This research employs quantitative secondary data collected from multiple data sources. The three main empirical chapters were estimated using system generalised method of moment (sys-GMM) for dynamic panel data analysis. The subsequent subsections describe each empirical chapter and its findings.

Research Conclusion on the Motivations of R&D FDI in the UK

The empirical analysis draws support from the strategic and specific motivation models initiated by Dunning (1998, 2002) and supported by Cantwell and Piscitello (2002, Von Zedtwitz and Gassmann (2002), Cantwell and Mudambi 2000 (2005), Zheng (2011), and Awate et al. (2015). Here, the study hypothesised that R&D FDI is similar to other traditional elements of the firm (e.g. production) and that it is likely to be driven by different motives as well. Adding to that, the hypothesis still follows that the OECD countries' specific motivation will have a higher magnitude (representing asset-exploitation and asset-augmentation strategic motivations) compared to non-OECD countries (representing asset-augmentation strategic motivations). Consistent with the study hypotheses, the empirical analysis revealed that market-seeking, efficiency-seeking, and strategic asset-seeking motivations are significant positive determinants of R&D FDI in the UK. This is, therefore, consistent with the economic theory of FDI motivations proposed by Dunning (1979, 1998, 2002, 2009).

The significant positive results for market-seeking motivation for the UK-pooled, OECD, and non-OECD countries corroborate with Kumar (2001), Athukorala and Kohpaiboon (2010), Belderbos et al. (2014), and Falk (2014), who provide empirical evidence that those locations with high income attract R&D FDI. Also seen in the empirical result is a higher coefficient estimate for market-seeking R&D FDI for OECD countries which indicates that countries with high per capita income and technological capabilities are more influenced by market-seeking motivation compared to countries with low per capita income and technological capabilities. This, therefore, suggests that MNEs from OECD countries with high technological capabilities and with pre-existing home-based competences are more attracted for market-seeking motivation than non-OECD countries. These findings draw support from market adaptation R&D FDI thesis in Dunning and Narula (1995) and Falk (2014).

The study finds that R&D FDI for UK country-level and OECD group are attracted by efficiency-seeking motivation (proxied by R&D personnel) and insignificant for the non-OECD group. These findings are consistent with extant literatures that argued that new products are multi-technology based and that firms with pre-existing capabilities would engage in both asset-augmenting and asset-exploiting strategies to sustain technology leadership (Bardhan 2006; Fifarek and Veloso 2010; Nieto and Rodríguez 2011; Awate et al. 2014; Zhou 2016). These authors suggest MNEs with pre-existing home-based competences will establish foreign R&D unit to allow the firms to focus on their core capabilities, for greater organisational flexibility and efficiency.

The study also finds that inward R&D FDI in the UK is attracted for strategic asset-seeking motivations (proxied by patent intensity) for all the models (pooled level, OECD, and non-OECD groups). These findings are consistent with Von Zedtwitz and Gassmann (2002), Iwasa and Odagiri (2004), and Di Minin et al. (2012) who showed that MNEs established R&D units abroad to gain access to crucial inputs such as new knowledge and technology that are location specific and are not easily available in their principal or home markets. Another explanation for this result draws support from the interaction of empirical results found for OECD and non-OECD country groups (as exhibited in Models II and III). The empirical result shows that specific and strategic motivations are different for OECD and non-OECD countries. For OECD countries, R&D FDI has a higher magnitude for market-seeking, efficiency-seeking, and strategic asset-seeking motivations which provide support for firms from home countries with advanced technological capabilities that may engage in both asset-exploiting and asset-augmenting strategies, while non-OECD countries' R&D FDI is for market-seeking and strategic asset-seeking which provide support from home countries with less technological capabilities that may tend to seek new knowledge for catch-up (asset-augmenting). This is consistent with Kuemmerle (1996, 1999) and Awate et al. (2014) that the strength of the location in science would influence the extent foreign affiliates to exploit existing firm-specific advantages and build up new firm-specific advantages or rather learn new knowledge to catch up and get on par with industry leaders.

Contributions to Knowledge and Theory

The main contributions of the study stem from the focus on a less-researched aspect of FDI, that is, R&D FDI, and its motivations in a particular developed country—the UK. Also, compared to previous literature, the study extends previous empirical studies on the motivations of inward R&D FDI in three main ways. First, unlike previous studies that have mainly examined the antecedents of strategic motivations at the subsidiary level and have ignored the specific motivations (like Cantwell and Piscitello 2002; Von Zedtwitz and Gassmann 2002; Cantwell and Mudambi 2000, 2005; Zheng 2011; Awate et al. 2015), this research conducts a country-level empirical analysis of inward R&D FDI in the UK. Second, the study further examines the similarity and distinction between the strategic and specific motivations of R&D FDI. Here, the study investigates the interactions of specific motivations (i.e. market-seeking, efficiency-seeking & strategic asset-seeking) to explain strategic motivations (home-based asset-exploitation and home-based asset-augmentation strategies) for inward R&D FDI in the UK. Third, the study tests the theoretical argument that, on the one hand, R&D FDI by MNEs with home-based capabilities will combine both asset-exploiting and asset-augmenting strategies (OECD countries), while, on the other hand, MNEs with no home-based capabilities will follow asset-augmenting strategy (non-OECD countries). This approach is consistent with Zheng (2013) in examining the variations in Indian inward FDI patterns and Zheng and Tan (2011) in examining home country heterogeneity in the determinants of China's inward FDI. However, unlike Zheng and Tan (2011) and Zheng (2013) who focused on aggregate FDI, this current study extends their approach to R&D FDI analysis. This approach allows for easy comparison of the study's empirical evidence, which provides greater insight into the similarity and dissimilarity of motivations among MNEs engaged in R&D FDI in the UK. These contributions have significant implications in corroborating prior theoretical and empirical literature on R&D internationalisation research stream.

Contribution to Practice

On the practical front, two key contributions are identified. First, the findings have policy implications for R&D FDI promotion agencies to adopt and implement selective or tailored promotions for desirable R&D FDI from specific home countries' groups. Here, national policy initiative should be centred on identifying R&D FDI from home countries with the good "fit" with existing national innovativeness and capability with the UK. However, due to the study findings that R&D FDI from OECD countries is accompanied with higher technological capabilities compared to non-OECD countries, policy measures (incentives) can be initiated to attract high value-adding R&D FDI into selective low-performing areas in the UK. Second, the findings also have managerial policy implications for corporate decision-makers. Here, decision-makers who wish to promote the overall corporate competitiveness and capabilities need to adopt a combination of specific motivations that reflect its strategic motives in the host location. For example, the study finds that OECD countries' R&D FDI in the UK is motivated for market-seeking, efficiency-seeking, and strategic asset-seeking in support of both asset-exploiting and asset-augmenting strategies given the higher magnitude of the estimated parameters, while non-OECD countries' R&D FDI is for market-seeking and strategic asset-seeking which provide support from home countries with less technological capabilities that may tend to seek new knowledge for catch-up (asset-augmenting).

Recommendations for Future Research

Although this study attempts to integrate certain idiosyncrasies at the country-level linked with MNEs' group/subsidiary-level behaviour, in an attempt to examine strategic and specific motivations R&D FDI, the study still has some limitations which also provide vital opportunities for future research. First, the study predominantly focused on R&D FDI motivations in a particular developed country—the UK. Future research might conduct a similar study on a large sample of host countries. Second, the empirical analysis was limited by the number of observations when the home countries were grouped into OECD and non-OECD countries with the OECD group' observations being higher than non-OECD by two- and half folds. However, this limitation is as a result of the eight countries removed in the analysis due to the fact that they are considered tax havens. Future research could overcome this by collecting data from a large sample of host countries. It would also be interesting for future research to investigate with wider coverage to incorporate other aspects, for example, politics, networking environment, and regional/supranational factors (see Fallon and Cook 2010, 2014). Such research would explain and refine existing theories and the motivations of R&D FDI across different locations on the motivations of R&D FDI.

Final Summary

In sum, this study reveals that R&D FDI in the UK is for market-seeking, efficiency-seeking, and strategic asset-seeking motivations. Also, this research reveals that different home countries' groups follow different strategic and specific motivations in their R&D FDI in the UK. The findings suggest that R&D FDI by OECD countries are influenced by market-seeking, efficiency-seeking, and strategic asset-seeking motivations which corroborate with the hypothesis that such MNEs with home-based assets usually combine both asset-exploiting and asset-augmenting strategies to gain complementary assets in the host location considered as a centre of excellence. When compared to the non-OECD countries' group, only market-seeking and strategic asset-seeking motivations are relevant, hence supporting asset-augmenting strategy.

References

Athukorala, P., & Kohpaiboon, A. (2010). Globalization of R&D by US-based multinational enterprises. *Research Policy, 39*(10), 1335–1347.

Awate, S., Larsen, M. M., & Mudambi, R. (2014). Accessing vs sourcing knowledge: A comparative study of R&D internationalization between emerging and advanced economy firms. *Journal of International Business Studies, 46*(1), 63–86.

Awate, S., Larsen, M. M., & Mudambi, R. (2015). Accessing vs sourcing knowledge: A comparative study of R&D internationalization between emerging and advanced economy firms. *Journal of International Business Studies, 46*(1), 63–86.

Bardhan, A. D. (2006). Managing globalization of R&D: Organizing for offshoring innovation. *Human Systems Management, 25*(2), 103–114.

Belderbos, R., Van Roy, V., Leten, B., & Thijs, B. (2014). Academic research strengths and multinational firms' foreign R&D location decisions: Evidence from R&D investments in European regions. *Environment and Planning A, 46*(4), 920–942.

Cantwell, J., & Mudambi, R. (2000). The location of MNE R&D Activity: The role of investment incentives. *MIR: Management International Review, 40*(1), 127–148.

Cantwell, J., & Mudambi, R. (2005). MNE competence-creating subsidiary mandates. *Strategic Management Journal, 26*(12), 1109–1128.

Cantwell, J., & Piscitello, L. (2002). The location of technological activities of MNCs in European regions: The role of spillovers and local competencies. *Journal of International Management, 8*(1), 69–96.

Di Minin, A., Zhang, J., & Gammeltoft, P. (2012). Chinese foreign direct investment in R&D in Europe: A new model of R&D internationalization? *European Management Journal, 30*(3), 189–203.

Dunning, J. H. (1979). Explaining Changing Patterns of International Production: In Defence of the Eclectic Theory: Explaining Changing Patterns of International Production. *Oxford Bulletin of Economics and Statistics, 41*(4), 269–295.

Dunning, J. H. (1998). Location and the multinational enterprise: A neglected factor? *Journal of International Business Studies, 1*(3), 45–66.

Dunning, J. H. (2002). *Global capitalism, FDI and competitiveness*. Cheltenham: Edward Elgar Publishing.

Dunning, J. H. (2009). Location and the multinational enterprise: John Dunning's thoughts on receiving the journal of international business studies 2008 decade award. *Journal of International Business Studies, 40*(1), 20–34.

Dunning, J. H., & Narula, R. (1995). The R&D activities of foreign firms in the United States. *International Studies of Management & Organization, 25*(1–2), 39–74.

Fallon, G., & Cook, M. (2010). Exploring the regional distribution of inbound foreign direct investment in the UK in theory and practice: Evidence from a five-region study. *Regional Studies, 44*(3), 337–353.

Fallon, G., & Cook, M. (2014). Explaining Manufacturing and Non-Manufacturing Inbound FDI Location in Five UK Regions. *Royal Dutch Geographical Society KNA, 105*(3), 331–348.

Falk, M. (2014). *Determinants of greenfield foreign direct investment in R&D and related activities*. FIW Research Reports Series no. IV-002.

Fifarek, B. J., & Veloso, F. M. (2010). Offshoring and the global geography of innovation. *Journal of Economic Geography, 10*(4), 559–578.

Iwasa, T., & Odagiri, H. (2004). Overseas R&D, knowledge sourcing, and patenting: An empirical study of Japanese R&D investment in the US. *Research Policy, 33*(5), 807–828.

Kuemmerle, W. (1996). Home base and foreign direct investment in R&D. Ph.D. Thesis: Harvard Business School.

Kuemmerle, W. (1999). Foreign direct investment in industrial research in the pharmaceutical and electronics industries-results from a survey of multinational firms. *Research Policy, 28*(2), 179–193.

Kumar, N. (2001). Determinants of location of overseas R&D activity of multinational enterprises: The case of US and Japanese corporations. *Research Policy, 30*(1), 159–174.

Nieto, M. J., & Rodríguez, A. (2011). Offshoring of R&D: Looking abroad to improve innovation performance. *Journal of International Business Studies, 42*(3), 345–361.

Von Zedtwitz, M., & Gassmann, O. (2002). Market versus technology drive in R&D internationalization: Four different patterns of managing research and development. *Research Policy, 31*(4), 569–588.

Zheng, P. (2011). The determinants of disparities in inward FDI flows to the three macro-regions of China. *Post-Communist Economies, 23*(02), 257–270.

Zheng, P. (2013). The variation in Indian inward FDI patterns. *Management International Review, 53*(6), 819–839.

Zheng, P., & Tan, H. (2011). Home economy heterogeneity in the determinants of China's inward foreign direct investment. *Transnational Corporations, 20*(2), 1–29.

Zhou, Y. (2016). Drivers of globalization of R&D investment by US multinational enterprises: Evidence from industry-level data. *International Journal of Economics and Finance, 8*(2), 51–69.

Index

O. Igbinigie et al., *Strategic Motivations of Inward R&D FDI*,
https://doi.org/10.1007/978-3-030-41015-5